BOYS BEHAVING BADLY

Jeremy Daldry was born in 1969. He lives by himself in West Hampstead, North London, with a classic car that doesn't work, a guitar he can't play and a signed picture of Groucho Marx.

He has worked as a freelance writer for a number of years on publications including *Arena, GQ, 19* and *The Readers Digest*. He's also been a regular columnist for both *The Daily Record* and the *Sunday Express*, as well as writing and presenting a number of TV shows including *Games World* and *Commercial Break* for Sky One and appearing regularly on *Gimme 5* and *GMTV*. He's also written *Total Reality* for the BBC and both series of *Love Bites* for LWT. *Boys Behaving Badly* is his first book.

what a boring sounding guy - what all this really means is that he gets up at lunch time and does 16 work!

EDDIE WAS BORN IN 1982. HE'S A NORMAL BLOKE, HE LIKES -NO-LOVES FOOTBALL, HANGS AROUND WITH HIS MATES AND THINKS THAT GIRLS SMELL NICE - EVEN IF THEY ARE A LITTLE WEIRD.

U.C. was also born in 1982. He is very cool, fashion god, babe magnet and owner of the largest collection of shades in the world. He is a dude!

BOYS BEHAVING BADLY

by Jeremy Daldry

with all the best bits
by J.C and EDDIE!

Piccadilly Press • London

Phototypeset from author's disk by Piccadilly Press.
Printed and bound by WBC, Bridgend
for the publishers Piccadilly Press Ltd.,
5 Castle Road, London NW1 8PR

A catalogue record for this book is available from the
British Library

ISBNs: 1 85340 451 9 (trade paperback)
1 85340 456 X (hardback)

Cover and inside design by Paul Cooper Design.

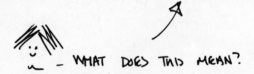

- WHAT DOES THIS MEAN?

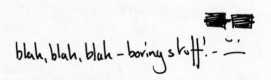

blah, blah, blah - boring stuff! -

who on earth are this lol? - I'd like to thank all the girls I've ever snogged. "

ACKNOWLEDGEMENTS:

There are so many people who have helped with this book, that to name them all would be impossible, however, thank you:

Mum and Dad – it's only because you did such a great job that I can write a book like this.

Stephen – for being the best brother and a dear friend.

Nick – for knowing when a beer is more important that a deadline. (Always.)

Ruth and Brenda – for knowing when a deadline is more important than a beer. (Always.)

Catherine – for her uncanny knowledge and understanding of young boys.

Greg at the BBC – for friendship, wise words and employment.

Matthew at LWT – for never letting me get away with things I shouldn't.

Eileen – for muppet dancing above and beyond the call of duty.

Alan Remy at the Daily Record – the best newspaper in the world and my boss for five years.

The Live and Kicking girls – Lucy, Annette and Suzanne. 'Another bottle of red, girls?'

THEY ALL SOUND VERY OLD!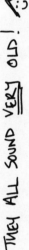

This book is dedicated,
with love and admiration,
to my father.

CONTENTS

INTRODUCTION

INTRODUCTION

**ARRRRRR!   What?   Where?   When?   Who?
WHAT'S HAPPENING TO ME?**

Deep breathe. Relax. Don't panic.

It's called being a teenager. ← *from outer-space!*

And it's perfectly normal.

And besides, that's why you (or someone else) have bought this **excellent,** and **remarkably good value,** book – to help answer those pesky, silly questions and offer you a user's guide to being a teenage bloke.

ALL RIGHT THEN! WHO SCORED THE WINNING GOAL IN THE 1978 FA CUP FINAL!

SO WHAT'S THIS BOOK ALL ABOUT, THEN?

Girls, mainly.

And – dates, kissing, conquests, dumping, being dumped, broken hearts, crushes, shaving, spots, greasy hair, farts, being smelly, willies, masturbation, wet dreams, girly mags, success, failure, depression, confidence, listening, talking, drink, drugs, peer pressure, bullying, fighting, parents, divorce, clothes, friends, money, death, brothers, sisters, step families.

Oh and **GIRLS**

it's not that cheap. I could have bought a new pair of shades instead!!

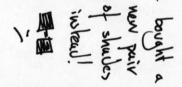

CHAPTER ONE

BOYS BEHAVING BADLY AROUND GIRLS

-SMELLY! STINKY! STINKY!

WHAT ARE GIRLS LIKE?

They are just great. There is something about them that is just so very squeezable.

you bet they are
I love girls

SHORT girls,

Tall girls,

U.C
all *girls*

fat girls...

thin girls,

they're all great. We love them.

But that doesn't stop girls being the cause of more
heartache
confusion and
AND FOOTBALL ———— **sleepless nights**
than almost anything else.

They might be wonderful – but they are also weird. All that giggling, drooling over boy bands and doing things with their nails and hair. What is *that* all about?

And as for trying to talk to them...

It's been scientifically proven that when any lad gets within two feet of a girl, she gives off a mysterious aura that turns normal bloke into gibbering wreck bloke who then can't string two words together.

normal
bloke

gibbering
wreck
bloke

It's proven. It's science. Strange but true.

WELCOME
TO THE
"X"
ZONE – WHERES MULLY AND SOULDER?

FLYING SAUCER

cool bloke

10

But you still *want* to talk to them.
You want to be *close* to them.
You want to *hold their hands,*
and go out on *dates with them.*

and kiss them
and cuddle them
and snog them
and snog them some
more

EEEK

I HATE THAT!

I'D RATHER HANG OUT WITH MY MATES!

And there lies a very **big** problem – asking " a girl out on a date.

Why, even when it's blooming obvious that a girl fancies the pants off you, do you find it so hard just to go up and ask them out?

I'll tell you why.

OH ER MRS!!

Because of the big **N.O.**

' of course no girl, no babe, no hot stuff ever says no to me.

Because of fear of rejection, or fear of the girl in question telling her mates, who then all have a good laugh about you.

But it shouldn't be scary, because, let's face it:

-never! I'm way too cool!

11

YOU PROBABLY KNOW WHEN
A GIRL WANTS TO BE ASKED OUT.

DO WE? – DOES SHE WEAR A TEE SHIRT?

ASK ME OUT!!

No, you do really.

There are those funny little signs. Like?

   ?

Well – when you talk to the babe in question...
• She blushes, or she starts
  to play with her hair.

I HATE IT WHEN GIRLS PLAY WITH THEIR HAIR – HAVE THEY ALL GOT NITS?

• She smiles when she sees you
coming and accidentally touches
you on the hand or leg when
you leave.

• She laughs at your naff jokes,
  asks loads of questions about
  you and then listens really
  closely to whatever
  you've got to say.

WHY DID THE CHICKEN CROSS THE ROAD?

TO GET TO THE OTHER SIDE!! –

BOOM, BOOM!!

There are loads and loads of little signs. You've just got to watch out for them.

— yes lets

But let's take a moment to think.

What is so wrong with a girl asking one of us lads out for a night on the town or a walk in the park? Nothing. Absolutely nothing. There is no rule that says that girls can't ask boys out. They should. It makes us feel wanted and means that for once us lads don't have to go through the 'pre' *ask out on a date*

hell.

So, if there are any **GIRLS** reading this book, take a hint:

ASK MORE BOYS OUT.
WE LIKE IT!

NE DO LIKE TO BE ASKED OUT AND STUFF — BUT YOU

But back to you and your potential date...

CAN'T BEAT GOING DOWN THE FOOTIE WITH YOUR MATES. GIRLS JUST DON'T UNDERSTAND FOOTBALL — THEY'VE GOT THEIR PONIES — BUT TRY AND GET THEM TO UNDERSTAND THE OFF SIDE RULE!

what's wrong with just going up to a girl and saying 'get your coat babe — you've pulled'?

ASKING A GIRL OUT

Here is a big tip – supposedly sure fire lines like:

'What's a beautiful girl like you doing in a place like this'?

CORNY

'Baby, it's your lucky day,' or

'How do you like your eggs in the morning?'

hey - these are all my best lines!

will only guarantee that you end up spending an awful lot of time *ON YOUR OWN*. Girls might want to be asked out, but they don't want to be insulted.

So there is nothing for it but to pluck up your courage, stride up to your favoured date target and say something like,

'Would you like to go out with me on Saturday night?'

Maybe it's not the most subtle of things to say but sometimes the direct approach is best.

OR SHOULD I JUST HANG OUT ON THE STREET CORNER WITH THE LADS?

I still prefer "baby it's your lucky day"

J.C © *copyright*

• HERE'S A SECRET •

You want to be a little sneaky about it?

Don't ask – suggest a date.

What's the difference?

Well, 'Want to go to the pictures with me,'
will get you a

WHAT?

YES

or

– always!!
no bube
could ever
resist me!!

NO

answer.

Which is great if the girl says YES
and a little less than great if she says NO.

But if you said,

*'I've got a couple of tickets for the
pictures, I though I might give you
one,'*

you're not forcing the issue, you're easing into it.
It's subtle, it's cute and it works.

BUT ISN'T THIS LIKE A TRICK?
OH – THAT'S THE POINT!
THAT'S CLEVER!

15

And before you ask – *think* about what you are going to do on your date.

snog!!

BUT WHAT IF YOU DON'T KNOW WHAT THEY LIKE TO DO ?

It's sometimes best, when you ask someone out, to give them some options, or at least give a hint at what the date might be. But if you plan your date in too much detail before you ask there isn't any flexibility to change your plans. So instead of...

1 - snog
2. snog
3 - snog
4 - snog
- it's simple

'I thought we could meet in town at 16.00 hours, inspect the local retail outlets until 16.45 hours and then retire to the moving picture complex to watch the 17.00 hours feature.'

You could try...

GIRLS AREN'T LIKE YOUR MATES... GIRLS ARE TOO STRANGE.

'If you like, we could meet in town at around 4 and then maybe catch a movie.'

Safer still is...

'Want to meet up in town at about 4 and then go on somewhere else?' – *and then snog?*

That will give you the chance to check out what's happening that afternoon and plan a few different things.

But it's always best to **remember** that there are **some basic asking out rules.**

girls always say YES to me ~~████~~ dude!

• It's NOT the best idea to go up to a girl when she is surrounded by her friends. *Even if* she is desperate for you to ask her out, she's going to be embarrassed if you ask and all her mates can overhear. And even more importantly, YOU will feel even worse if she says NO.

• GET to the point. Don't 'ummm' and 'arrrr'. Don't spend hours leading up to asking her out. Say, 'hi', ask her how she's doing and then come out with,

> *If you're free on Saturday night...*

AFTER THE FOOTIE OF COURSE!!

• **Don't, don't, don't**

get a friend to ask for you. That's just so tacky. Remember that you are asking a girl out because you want to be with her – no other reason. If you get a friend to ask her out, it looks like you don't really care that much whether she says YES or NO *and* it makes you look like a COMPLETE COWARD. Also, your friend might move in on your date and ask her out himself.

LET'S HAVE A DATE BABE!

(IF I'M NOT DOING ANYTHING WITH THE LADS)

RING **RING** **RING** **RING**

And for those of you who really want to go for the safe option you just need a phone.

← a phone

Some people are more relaxed on the phone.

↘ it's good to talk hu, hu, hu

They find it easier to talk. Can't face the girl in the flesh? Phone them.

But don't BLURT it out and don't TAKE FOREVER to get to the point. Why not write a few notes deciding what you want to say before you say it. It's not dorky and no one will be able to tell.

Then just pick a good time to phone:

6AM – **not too early in the morning**

11.30 PM – **not too late at night**

"NIGHT OF THE KILLER BUNNIES" – **not when there is a great movie on TV which they might be watching, and**

GO FOR IT

– of course I'll go out with you J.C. Give us a snog!

– ok babe!

But if you do use the phone, remember to ask to speak to your potential date and say who's calling. People can sound different on the phone and you don't want this to happen:

'**Hi Helen, I was just wondering if you'd like to go out to the pictures with me on Saturday?**'

'**I think you want to speak to my daughter.**' ⇒ fancy a date

'**Oh sorry. Yes please.**' Helen's mum?

(**Embarrassing pause.**)

EMBARRASSING PAUSE ✱

'**Hi, this is Helen.**'

'**Hi Helen, I was just wondering if you'd like to go out to the pictures with me on Saturday?**'

'**That would be nice – but who are you?**' || - Johnny Cool "Super Stud".

Not the best way to start a date.

It's really simple: *you* want to ask, *your* date probably wants to be asked. So, take your time, get to know the person, smile, be confident, walk up to her and ask her out.

HELLO GIRL... ERM...
FANCY A DATE?

19

WHAT TO DO IF SHE SAYS NO

yer-right thats really going to happen!!!

If the girl in question does say,

'Thanks, but no thanks,'

OR SHE MIGHT SAY "HOP OFF AND DIE"

there is no point pleading, getting down on your knees or getting all huffy about it. If you ask someone out, they have the right to say no.

DON'T

TAKE IT PERSONALLY,

DON'T

GET DEPRESSED BY IT *and*

DON'T

GO OFF IN A STROP.

but if you never ask - you'll never know and you'll never snog! And that would be a tragedy!

It happens to everyone. You'll get over it. Sometimes you'll get knocked back and that can be annoying. Even the biggest dude in the entire world will have been rejected sometimes. But if you never ask you'll never know and you could be missing out on some

red hot dates.

NO WORRIES - JUST GIVE HER THE OLD ELBOW AND HAVE A FUN SATURDAY NIGHT TALKING FOOTBALL. WHO NEEDS GIRLS?

THE DATE

Ok – so you managed to pluck up enough courage to actually ask the girl of your dreams out on a date. But now you've actually got to GO ON THE DATE.

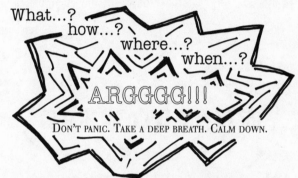

What...? how...? where...? when...?

ARGGGG!!!

Don't panic. Take a deep breath. Calm down.

The D-Day landings can seem simple compared to planning a good first date. But don't worry because

it's really simple.

And remember – you're not the only one being farty about the whole thing. She will almost certainly be going through exactly the same stomach turning, last minute panic.

YER-RIGHT!

STINKY!!
WHO LET ONE
DROP?

HELLO. IM A
STOMACH TURNING.

U's RED HOT DATE

1- snog hello, 2- pictures (snogging in the dark), 3- walk home (with occasional snog), 4- snog goodnight.

STINKY POOH SMELLY

WASHING IS FOR GIRLS!

I NEVER WASH.

Everyone thinks it's just girls who spend all day preparing for dates. No way!

We've all done it: sat there trying to decide what to wear, spent so long in the bathroom that your mum comes and knocks on the door and says if you don't stop whatever you're doing you'll go blind, and even stealing some of your dad's aftershave so you smell like a

lurve god.

And that's before you even get to leave the house!

So first big decision: ? ? ? ? ? ? ? ? ? ? someone call?

WHAT TO WEAR

? ? ? ? ? ? ? ?

OK, LET'S START WITH:

WHAT NOT TO WEAR

Jc's hot fashion tips

- There is no point borrowing your brother's latest club gear because if you get as far as a second date your potential girlfriend might expect you to wear something equally hip. Also if you 'borrow' something from your older brother without asking him you might have to go on your date minus the hip gear but with a black eye.

1- always wear your shades - even at night and inside.

2. dowse yourself in aftershave 'LA STUD' is good.

3- never leave the house without your trousers.

HE.HE.HE

EEK! I FORGOT MY PANTS!

22

TEE SHIRT, 4 WEEKS OLD -
RIPPED
UEANS - OLD
TRAINERS
WITH HOLES
IN THE TOE -
HOW MUCH
MORE COOL
CAN
YOU
GET
?
.

- Don't buy something new. If you blow all your cash on a new outfit and then next time you see your date you look like an old scruff bag you'll look stupid.

- Don't wear a tie. I mean come on, a tie! You're not going to your cousin's wedding.*

* Unless, of course,
  your date is at your
  cousin's wedding
  – then maybe a tie might
  be quite a good idea.

this tie
is
NOT
mmm
funny.

Good things to wear

It's important that you feel comfortable but you also want to look like you care – like you've made an effort to make yourself look good for your date.

DOES
THAT
MEAN
YOU DO
GIRLIE STUFF...
LIKE
WASH
YOUR
FEET?

Yuk

But...

remember, you should always wear something that makes **YOU** feel comfortable. Smart, scruffy, whatever... as long as it's **YOU** it really shouldn't matter. Remember, she's going on a date with **YOU**, not your wardrobe.

fancy a date?

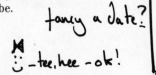

- tee. hee - ok!

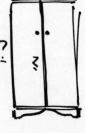

So that's the clothes sorted. And while we are on the subject of things to wear and not to wear, let's talk about aftershave.

OUCH, OUCH
TOO
LATE!!!
THAT
STINGS...
BUT I CAN
TAKE IT...
I'M A
REAL
MAN.
OUCH.
  OUCH
  OUCH.

HALF A BOTTLE OF BRUT DOWN YOUR BOXERS DOES **NOT** SMELL GOOD. IT WILL ALSO HURT LIKE HELL, SO DON'T DO IT.

FISH
FEET
POO
STINK
POO

STUD

AS WORN BY
U.C. SUPER STUD

Girls like you to smell nice, so wash your feet, but they don't like you to smell like the perfume counter of Boots, so remember a little goes a long way.

So you smell nice, you look cool, everything is great. Let's get on to the date itself.

24

— lots of snogging?

HOW TO BEHAVE ON THE DATE

You might know this girl really well – she might be your best friend – but you've never been on a date with her before. And dates are *different*. Don't ask me why, they just are. You've asked a girl out...

PANIC - PANIC
PANIC - PANIC

TO BE WITH YOU. ALONE. BECAUSE YOU LIKE HER.

But remember: calm, calm, calm. You have asked a girl out on a date and she has said **YES.**
She wants to be there.
She wants to be with you.
She must like you at least a little.
Not a bad place to start a date from.

— or a lot if she is going out with me!

THIS LONG

GOLDEN RULE NUMBER ONE:
FIRST IMPRESSIONS COUNT.

THINGS TO DO: *I do a great Donald Duck*

1. BE ON TIME *quack, quack, flup, flup - good isn't it?*
You've asked her out and it will *not* go down well if you are late.

But what if the girl you have asked out is late?
Well it's only polite to wait a while. You never know – she might have been held up or missed her bus.
But how long should you wait? And what should you do while you are waiting?

U.C with a beak!

➤ DO LIKE ME - GIVE HER A COUPLE OF MINUTES AND THEN HEAD OFF TO THE CHIP SHOP WITH YOUR MATES FOR A PICKLED EGG FIGHT!!

stood up

20 minutes is about the minimum you should wait – although if you are keen on the girl you might find yourself kicking your heels for at least an hour. If you have arranged to meet someone it's usually a good idea to have a book or a magazine with you, and then if they are late you can read. There is nothing worse than waiting on a street corner for someone and feeling like everyone knows you are waiting on a street corner for someone.

An HOUR! You've GOT TO BE PULLING MY LEG!!

Snug?!

2. HAVE AN IDEA WHERE TO GO
Ideally you will have already covered what you are going to do on your date when you asked her out, but if you didn't, have at least a couple of suggestions up your sleeve.

something that never, ever happens to J.C. – because he is such a cool dude type bloke!

You DON'T want this to happen:

You:
   What you want to do?'
Your date:'
   Dunno, what do you want to do?'
You:
   Whatever.'
Your date:'
   I don't mind, whatever you feel like.'
You:'
   I'm easy. It's up to you.'
Your date:
   Whatever. You pick.'
You:
Nar you.'

HEY! HOW DID THEY KNOW WHAT HAPPENS WHEN I GO OUT ON A DATE?

26

I mean please. Something like this
might be a little better:

You:
  What do you want to do?'

Your date:
  ' I don't know, what do you want to do?'

You:
  *'Well, we could check out the latest Jim
  Carey movie or go for a walk in the park
  or just wander round the shops.'*

*What a
dull date.*

Your date:
  'The movies sound great.'

You:
  'Lovely.'

Your date:
  *'Super'**

*Go out with J.C.
super stud and its fun.
fun, fun all the way.
Just because I'm around. And
that's guaranteed.*

*OH I SAY —
WOULD ONE
LIKE TO BE
GOING ON A
DATE WITH ONE??
WHAT? TOP HOLE!*

*if you really talk like this you are:

A – straight out of some weird
   Famous Five book

B – in need of more help than this
   little book can offer

C – Prince William ???

Another way of tackling the whole, 'what to do?' thing
might be to let your date choose.

**ALWAYS REMEMBER:
YOU ASKED HER OUT.**

*POSH
EDDIE*

*unless - of course - the babe
in question asked me out!*

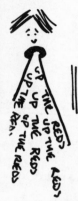

If she doesn't mind and leaves it up to you then pick something you will both enjoy.

First dates that take place in the home supporters' stand of your local football club are usually also last dates. Unless, of course, your date is a big footie fan.

Movies are a pretty good bet. There is probably something on that you would both like to see and it also means that you can spend time together without having to talk.

- No embarrassing pauses in conversation.
- No trying to think of what to say next.
- And you'll have something to talk about afterwards.

But *remember*, just because you want to see

Death Nuns in Chainsaw Hell 3 – Revenge of the Wimple

your date might not want to. Ask her what she would like to see.

3. LET'S TALK ABOUT TALKING

Whatever you do – you are going to have to talk to your date at some point.

IT CAN'T BE HELPED – THAT'S WHAT DATES ARE ALL ABOUT. Talking to a date might seen a little daunting. It can be difficult, it can seem embarrassing, you might think you are sounding stupid. And nerves can get the better of you.

handwritten marginalia: UP THE REDS, UP UP THE REDS, UP UP THE REDS, UP THE REDS

handwritten marginalia: "A CLASSIC MOVIE – BUT NOT AS GOOD AS "MUTANT TOXIC BIKINI GIRLS GO SPLAT"

handwritten marginalia: and there is always the back row for a quick snog

handwritten marginalia: blah. blah. blah. blah. blah. blah. blah. blah. blah. blah. blah. blah. blah. blah. blah. funny or sexy?

You might want to say,

'That was a good film, wasn't it?'

But what might come out is,

WIBBLE, YIPPLE, PIPPLE, PONG, BELCH.'

NO REALLY!!!

(swawkcab)

Just relax. Here's a secret – GIRLS ARE PEOPLE TOO. They will forgive you if you get your words backwards or if you make a bad joke. They are as nervous as you are.

But if you are worried about those

← 1 ʍʍo ʍʍn ʍʍg →

embarrassing pauses just remember to follow a few simple rules.

– you haven't been listening to anything I've said!!

A. Listen to what she is saying. There is no point thinking up something very witty to say if you haven't been paying any attention to what *she* has been saying.

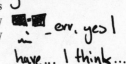

– err, yes I have... I think... erm.

B. Don't bore her either. The whole point of a good conversation is that it goes two ways. She isn't out with you to be lectured at about...
– Why Ryan Giggs is a footballing god,
– How Liam Gallagher is a prat, or,
– Why Pam Anderson is every boys perfect girl.

BLAH. BLAH
BLAH. BLAH
BLAH. BLAH
BLAH. BLAH
BLAH. BLAH, BLAH
BLAH. BLAH, BLAH
BLAH. BLAH. BLAH. BLAH
BLAH. BLAH. BLAH. BLAH.
BLAH. BLAH. BLAH. BLAH...
HELLO? HELLO!

C.   Ask her questions. Most people like, and are good at, talking about themselves. It will also make you look like you are interested in her and want to find out more. It's also a good idea to ask questions that don't just require a 'yes', or 'no' answer. So asking,

I'm good at talking about myself – I'm so fantastic!

dude!

'Which bit of the movie did you like best?'

is better than asking,

'It was a good movie, wasn't it?'

D.Don't go on and on and on and on and on and on about yourself. It's fine to drop in little things about yourself, but don't sit down and tell her your life story – unless, of course, she asks.

I WAS BORN ON A DARK AND STORMY NIGHT. I LOVE FOOTIE – LET ME TELL YOU ABOUT THE CLASSIC 4-4-2 FORMATION – IT'S JUST SO COOL... BLAH, BLAH, BLAH.

E. Every conversation has some silences. You don't have to rush to fill every breath with a joke or a story.

YAWN!

A SILENCE

30

F.

OH – SURE... THAT'S EASY FOR YOU TO SAY.

Relax.

4. Money... cash, wonga, dosh, moula

This is a tough one. No girl should expect you to pay for everything. If you want to pay for your date that's fine – that's your privilege but no girl should expect it to be her right.

If you are going to the movies you might want to offer to pay – most girls will then pick up a pizza afterwards or buy some popcorn.

Don't, don't, don't tell a girl you would like to take her out and then turn up skint and have to resort to a hot date sitting in a bus shelter. If you've got no cash then let her know subtly when you ask her out. Suggest a walk in the park and an ice cream – cheap, cool and pretty romantic.

THE BEST WAY TO GET OUT OF SPENDING ANY DOSH IS TO ORDER LOADS OF FOOD AT McBURGER – PRETEND YOU'RE GOING TO PAY AND THEN SAY "SORRY BABE – I FORGOT MY CASH". THEN YOUR DATE WILL HAVE TO BUY YOU THE FOOD!

REMEMBER – YOU DON'T HAVE TO HAVE GREAT WADS OF CASH TO GO ON A GOOD DATE.

5. Don't forget you are on a date with her

If you run into some mates, don't go off with them and ignore your date. However, if you do see someone you know, don't try and hide the fact you are on the date.

If you act like you are embarrassed to be with your date, it will probably be your last date with her. But don't parade her around either. She isn't a trophy or a new pair of trainers for your mates to admire and pass comments on.

Do any of these and you will, to be frank, look like a prat. And your date will hate it.

OH! ISN'T SUE?

ANYWAY I ONLY LIKE GIRLS WHO LOOK LIKE PAMELA ANDERSON'

my date — the paper bag girl.

6. Do offer to walk your date home

It's only polite and shows that you care that she gets home OK.

But if she says she'll be Ok, don't, don't, don't make a big song and dance about how dangerous the streets are and how you must protect her.

but who's the Green Goblin?

You're not Superman, she's not Lois Lane. The days of knights in shinning armour are long gone. Girls can look after themselves.

NICE
LOVELY
super
Great
wonderful

so everything has gone well, you've had a great date.
She's...

- *laughed* at your jokes,
- *listened* to your stories,
- *enjoyed* the movie and
- *shared* a milkshake in McDonald's.

You are a success. The date is a success. But now comes
the biggest problem of all...

*of course... I'm J.C.
after all.*

I HATE
THIS BIT.
WHAT IF
HER
BREATH
SMELLS, OUR
TEETH CLINK
OR NOSES
GET ALL
CRUSHED?

the kiss goodnight

WOW – that is always a real toughie...

when?
Where?
how?
Tongues or no tongues?

at last snogs!

BUT DON'T PANIC:

the kiss goodnight can be really nice and
not as nerve wracking as you might think.

U.C's top snogging tip
1- take the gum out of your mouth
2- blow your nose

The difficult thing about the kiss goodnight is that someone has to make the first move, otherwise you'll never get round to touching lips or tickling tongues.

no problem.

I'm in like a shot for some tongue tango action.

So this is the scene:

the date's been great and you've
walked the babe to her bus stop
or her house.
And then you stop.
You say thanks for coming. *- "thanks"*
Your date says thanks for a great *- "you're great J.C"*
time.
You both stand and do a swirly,
twisty little dance on the spot.
You both look at each other. *- "I know...*
You both giggle a little and then... *give us a snog"*

I JUST GRAB THEM. CLOSE MY EYES, PRESS MY ***nothing***
LIPS AGAINST THEM AND HOPE FOR THE BEST

But that's where a kiss should come in.
So what do you do?
   Well, while you are giggling and twirling you could reach out your hand. Your date then might understand what you are trying to do and take it.

34

buzz zip zing crackle

Wow – you've touched. Pretty electric stuff.

And then just let your hand, still holding hers, fall to your side. Now unless you've both got incredibly

STRETCHY

arms you're going to have to move closer together.

We are not talking about you pulling someone to you like a fish on the end of a rod – just letting your hand and arm suggest a movement that gets your date closer to you.

EEK!

what, you mean like this?

THAT'S CLOSE

How close? About the length of your lips.

😠 – kiss kiss

Now is the time for courage. Now is the time for snogs!

The time for the **kiss**.

Reach in gently and plant a delicate kiss on your date's lips or, if you want to take it slower, her cheek.

You'll then know 100%, dead certain, whether or not she wants you to kiss her again, because if she does she'll

BORING

THIS MAKES IT ALL SOUND SO VERY BORING!

kiss. you back. — of course she will.

A KISS SHOULD JUST LAST 3 SECONDS!!

It's all very simple, the key is reading the signals – those little signals that let you know when the time is right and whether your date wants to be kissed at all.

All the:

- *giggling,* — hee. hee, har, har give me a snog
  J.C.
- *looking in each other's eyes,*
- *holding hands,*
- *gently touching each others' arms or backs.*
    Little things like these. And when you get to the moment of truth you'll find:
- *your face very close to hers,*
- *yourself looking into each other's eyes,*
- *that the conversation has dried up,*
- *you both glancing at each other's mouth,*
- *yourself kissing.* — the moment of truth — the snog

Wow.

Yippee.

Home Run.

Houston – we have touched down.

WHAT IF WHEN YOU GET TO THIS STAGE, INCHES FROM A GIRL, YOU DO A

BIG, SMELLY CHEESE AND ONION CRISP FLAVOURED BURP?

=don't be silly - all girls love me!

HOWEVER, if there isn't any giggling, your date is walking quickly ahead of you with her arms crossed and any conversation is of the, 'Yes', 'No', variety then there probably isn't going to be a kiss.

Don't take it personally – sometimes dates just don't work out. If that's the case it's time to bow out and admit that it wasn't meant to be. No hard feelings.

Or perhaps your date just doesn't feel ready to kiss you yet. If you've obviously got on well then it probably means she'd still like to go on another date. Remember to read those signs. Each situation is different.

I could never, ever, ever, EVER date a girl who didn't like footie.

But let's say that the date is a success and the kiss is fast looming. We get to that eternal question:

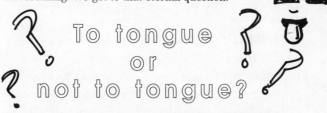

To tongue
or
not to tongue?

Sometimes people like to kiss with their mouths open and use their tongues to explore each other's mouths. As gross as that sounds, it actually feels very nice, although it isn't everyone's cup of tea and it might take a little bit of getting used to. It's called

French kissing – although it's got nothing to do with the French. If you don't want to French kiss or your date doesn't want to, then there is no rule that says you have to.

Je t'aime. wee. wee - fancy a la snogette? *oh J.C you are so french.*

Kissing isn't a simple matter of **A, B, C.**

choice!!

It's a wonderful thing

Sometimes a quick *LIP LOCK* is wonderful, sometimes an end of the world *SLUPPY SNOG* is the only thing that will do.

But on your first kiss goodnight, it's probably best to err on the side of caution. If you both want to get the tongues going – fine. But if not, that's fine too.

Just remember that there are some basic kissing rules that apply just as well for the first kiss goodnight or for any other time you kiss a girl.

I very often have to choose which babe to snog.

• **Don't** lunge at the girl as if you are trying to rugby tackle her.

YUK!!. THAT'S HORRIBLE – BUT FUNNY!

• **Don't** try and force your tongue as far down her throat as it will go. You're kissing, not trying to find out what she had for lunch.

• **Don't** assume just because you've been out on a date that you have the right to kiss her. You don't. And your date doesn't have the right to kiss you or expect you to kiss her.

• **Don't** assume just because you've had a quick kiss that things are automatically going to go further.

• **Don't** burp while you are kissing. That's too gross.

snog me first J.C.

no snog me

snog me

OR YOUR NOSE!!

• **Do** pick your place – somewhere that isn't too busy and where neither her, nor your, friends will suddenly make an appearance.

• **Do** make sure, if it's outside your date's house, that her parents can't see. She might feel uncomfortable about having a quick snog with her mum watching through the windows.

• **Do** take your time.

• **Do** enjoy it.

but of course - kissing is great and I'm the best. the girls always come back

Dates can be a nightmare,

for move from me.

YEAH!!

but they don't have to be. From asking a girl out to kissing her goodnight, the key to the whole thing is to take your time, be yourself and never ever forget that you are with another person – not a cardboard cut-out

SOMETIMES

but a real person who has feelings, emotions and interests just like you.

SHE DOESN'T LOOK LIKE PAMMY A' WHICH IS A SHAME BECAUSE I'M SO HANDSOME.

Talk to your date.

Get to know her.

Share a few little secrets.

The whole point of a date is that you are trying someone on for size – seeing if they fit, seeing if you hit it off, seeing if you like each other enough to go on another date and another and another.

WHAT IF IT GOES BANANA SHAPE? HA, HA.

IF IT ALL GOES PEAR-SHAPED – DON'T WORRY ABOUT IT.

a pear-shaped date? now that's weird.

It happens. Sometimes two people who should get on like a house on fire can't stand each other after they've spent some time together alone.

Just ⤳ move ⤳ on.

Always remember that every great romantic duo, every old married couple and every film star, rock god or super model has all had first dates.

Relax – enjoy them.

dates are great! girls are great :) snogs are great! everyone loves J.C.

the next step

THE NEXT STEP

The date has gone great.

You had a snog goodnight.

You are proud as punch because..

A GIRL LIKES YOU.

but of course she does... I'm JC... super stud.

40

thank you very much!

EXCELLENT. WELL DONE.

it was nothing really.

NOW WHAT?

Well, going into school the next day and telling all your mates that you got off with so and so from Year Nine is a big

no-no. YES·YES

_BUT ALL MY MATES LOVE HEARING ABOUT ANY GIRLS I GET OFF WITH.

why?

Look, just think about it for a minute.

It's natural to feel great if you have got it together with someone – you feel happy and even proud. ☺

It's natural to want to tell as many people as possible so they all know how happy you are and maybe even so you can brag about it a little bit.

But, remember that you are talking about

SOMEONE ELSE –
and someone else who you supposedly like.

J.C Golden Rule - always exaggerate how far you got with a girl you ~~don't~~ want your mates to think you're a wimp!

41

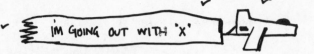

I'M GOING OUT WITH 'X'

The other person might not want the
whole school,
youth club,
world to know that you had a quick
snog in the park and that you tried to put your hand up
her jumper.

> OH ER MRS. WHERE'S MY TROUSERS VICAR?

If you get off with someone it's always
best to assume that they want to keep it a
secret. When you first start seeing a girl,
when you first become an item, it takes a
little while for you both to get used to the
idea.

It takes a while for you to stop going,

> but for how long
> an hour, a day,
> a week?
> anyway any girls
> that I see
> want every-
> one to
> know they
> are
> dating J.C

'Struth. I am actually going out with her. I can't believe it.'

And oddly enough, that's why when we first start dating
someone we want to tell other people – because it
makes it all seem more real to us.

CONFUSED?
It's simple.

A. You go out on a date with Little Miss Gorgeous.
B. You and LMG get off with each other.
C. You and LMG decide to become an item. You are
boyfriend and girlfriend. It's official.

> Little Miss Gorgeous? I think I dated
> her for a while.

D. You can't believe that you and LMG are going out
    – because she is gorgeous.

E. You tell all your friends about going out with LMG
    because that makes it more real. If your mates
    know it must be true.

F. LMG dumps you, because she didn't want anyone
    to know right away.

B u m m e r

CATCH 22

(FART)

ME ME ME.

– POP!

If you really are bursting to tell someone then
just tell one friend who you can trust not to
spread the news around. Better still, write it
down in a diary or a letter to yourself.

HEY!!
THAT'S
MY
LETTER!

Dear Me,
I'm going out with a gorgeous girl.
She is gorgeous.
I can't believe it – but now I've
written it down it must be true. Wow.
    Yours
    Me

hey!!
that's
my
letter!

SIMPLE.

LIKE ME! DOH!

43

So once you've both got used to the idea that you are an item then it might be nice to let people know that you are a couple. You don't have to take out an advert in the local paper, just hold hands in public, be seen together, snuggle together.

People will get the idea.

However, if you are with someone and after a few weeks or even a few months they still don't want people to know that you are together, then it might be a good idea to ask why they don't.

Just as it's not natural to rush out and put up fly posters announcing that you're an item, it's also

not natural never to tell anyone.

It might mean that they aren't happy about something, they might feel a little embarrassed, they might just be very shy. Not everyone likes to live their private lives in public.

If you want to go public and they don't, sit and talk about it. There is probably a

very good reason.

buzz, crackle... this is Radio 4 with an important news flash. J.C has got a new babe... we repeat J.C has got a new girlfriend.

BOYS BEHAVING BADLY AROUND GIRLS

Remember, talking is the best thing you can ever do with a girl. Well maybe not the best thing – but we talk about that later. — *phwoar. nudge. nudge. wink. wink say no more*

love

HOW do you know when you fall in love with someone?

That is not a simple question to answer.

Various poets, writers and singers have spent hundreds of years trying to say what it is that makes

love, love,

what it is that makes us feel so very much for one particular person, what it is that makes us want to **laugh, sing** and **dance** every time that we see that person and cuddle up in a ball and **cry** when we don't.

Who can tell?

Sometimes you are with someone and you just know.

-sniff... love is in the air... can't you smell it... either that or someones just dropped one!

BUT THATS WHAT HAPPENS TO ME EVERYTIME MY FOOTIE TEAM SCORES

ever fallen in love with someone you shouldn't? all the girls fall for me!

45

You look at them and you just know that they are a person you don't want to be without.

= YES IT CAN!

Love is not something that can be put into words.

Love is not easy – it's not straightforward.

There are absolutely no rules about falling in love with someone.

DOESN'T THE OFF SIDE RULE APPLY? THE EXTRA TIME PENALTY SHOOT OUT? OH... THAT'S A SHAME.

You can meet someone and after a couple of hours you love them completely or you can be friends with a person for years and years and then suddenly wake up one day and discover that you've fallen head over heels in love with them.

However, there are certain things that love isn't about:

It isn't about controlling someone or getting them to do something they don't want to do.

It isn't about saying, 'I love you,' just to get a girl to sleep with you.

It isn't about trying to change a person to make them into the kind of girl you want them to be.

WHAT LIKE THE WONDERFUL PAMMY ANDERSON? SO PRETTY... AND SO CLEVER!

poet JC

roses are red, violets are blue, you are great, so give us a snog!

SO WHY DO GIRLS FIND IT SO EASY?

I LOVE YOU!

Saying, 'I love you' can be tough.

Admitting that someone matters that much to you is a particularly tough thing for us lads to manage.

BUT IT'S IMPORTANT. *Why?*

Well, just imagine you are with a girl who you love. You can't help it. You've just fallen head over heels, gob smackingly, end of the world in love with her.

That's great.

But now you want to tell her.

That isn't so great. There are all the worries and fears that she is going to:

YUP — **a - laugh**

OH YES — **b - slap you or**

VERY PROBABLY — **c - go, 'What did you say?'**

But very few girls will do any of the above.

When someone tells you that they love you, it's obvious that they are laying themselves on the line. They are being very honest and open about their feelings and only the most heartless girl in the world would laugh at you after you've told her something so personal.

J:s top love tip

don't confuse LOVE and LUST. They are different. the girls have this problem with me.

So the only thing that you can do is...

trust to your judgement and pick the right time to let her know just how you feel.

MY JUDGEMENT ISN'T VERY GOOD – ID RATHER WAIT FOR MY MATES TO TELL ME.

So don't tell her,
- over the phone
- in a letter
- just as you are saying goodnight
- after an argument
- when she is surrounded by her friends
- in the cinema.

Tell her somewhere that is private, but don't build the whole thing up and don't, don't, don't, go down on one knee.

You're not proposing.

Just come out with it. Just say, '

I love you.

Simple.

However, don't expect her to say, 'I love you,' back. That isn't why you told her, and besides, having someone tell

48

you that they have fallen in love with you can be something of a shock – she probably needs a little time to get over it and have a think about what you've just said.

You hope she feel the same but unfortunately it doesn't always work out like that.

REALL!! ⟹

OH-OH

So what can you do if the girl of your dreams, who you have just declared your undying love to turns round and says,

'That's very sweet, but I *don't love* you.'

✳-does that happen? not with U.C. supa stuu.

Not much I'm afraid.

You've just got to get up, dust yourself down and accept it. There is no point getting angry, bitter or aggressive. There is no point trying to win her over with love letters, flowers or gifts. There is no point trying to make someone love you.

It doesn't work that way.

The only thing that you can do is accept it and feel sad. *AND GO BACK TO THE FOOTIE!*

HOW DO YOU KNOW IT'S LOVE?

One way of being sure that you really do love someone before you tell them is to sit yourself down and ask yourself some questions.

SHOULD I COMPARE THEE TO A SUMMER'S DAY
HOT, STICKY AND SURROUNDED BY FLYS.
EDDIE-SPEARE © 97

sad *happy* *in love*

49

ME	**'Do I love this girl? '**
ME 2	*'Yes. I think so.'*
ME	**'Are you sure Me 2?'**
ME 2	*'Well – I think I'm sure.'*
ME	**'Do you think about her a lot?'**
ME 2	*'All the time. I can't think of anything else.'*
ME	**'Do you long to be with her?'**
ME 2	*'Oh yes. She's great, she makes me feel kind of whole and special.'*
ME	**'Would you feel absolutely devastated if she dumped you?'**
ME 2	*'Do cheese and onion crisps make your breath smell like the inside of a jock strap?'*
ME	**'Do you fancy her more than Pamela Anderson?'**
ME 2	*'Pamela who?'*
ME	**'Maybe you've got a crush on her?'**
ME 2	*'Maybe. But I really know her and I think it's more than that. I love her.'*
ME	**'You sure you're sure?'**
ME 2	*'Yes. Yes, I am.'*
ME	**'Great. She is gorgeous.'**
ME 2	*'She is, isn't she?'*

SHOCKED EDDIE ↓

HE → MUST BE IN LOVE!

I wouldn't know – I never eat old Jock straps

what's her number?

& 'Yuk!'

ISNT MOUNT HONESTY SOMEWHERE IN SCOTLAND?

If you are being honest with yourself you probably all know in your heart of hearts whether you are really in love with someone or just fancy them or have got a crush on them, because one thing that love does demand is mountains of honesty.

MOUNT HONESTY FIRST CLIMBED BY EDDIE! (THIS IS A LIE!)

U -YUM!

Sometimes it's nice to think you are in love, or con yourself into thinking that you are in love because there is nothing nicer.

CHEESE BURGER WITH A FRIED EGG, DOUBLE CHIPS, PEAS AND A MUG OF TEA IS BETTER!

There is nothing nicer than feeling that safe and that wanted.

It's an easy mistake to make – you just have to look into your heart and decide that what you feel really is

true love.

YOU'RE GREAT U.C - I LOVE YOU!

When you are in love with someone you have to be honest to yourself and to that person. It's tough – but that's the deal. *– it's not tough for me – the girls all tell me how very wonderful I am.*

So what about crushes?

What's the difference between being in love and having a crush? And how can we not mistake one for the other?

I'VE GOT A CRUSH - BOOM, BOOM.

Well, a crush is like falling in love with someone that you know you'll never get it together with or someone who you don't know at all. They might be your teacher, a rock star, a super model or just someone in your class.

Crushes are usually fairly intense and the person you've got the crush on is all you can think about for a while.

in tents!! get it?

But it isn't **love.**

WHAT IS IT THEN?

In fact, if you and the object of your crushdom ever did get it together you'd probably be massively disappointed.

Crushes are also a big part of the way that you get to understand your own particular sexuality.

THIS DOESN'T SOUND LIKE A LOT OF LAUGHS - I THINK I'LL STICK TO THE FOOTIE!

→ **WHEN YOU HIT PUBERTY IT'S NOT JUST YOUR BODY THAT CHANGES, BUT IT'S YOUR MIND AND FEELINGS THAT UNDERGO A PRETTY MASSIVE UPHEAVAL TOO.**

You become aware of your own sexuality, you become much more aware of girls and you start feeling **attracted towards them**. At first it isn't always possible to understand these feelings and they can be confusing. Often you find yourself developing a crush on someone. It's usually someone older – like a teacher or a pop star.

certainly do! and they start feeling attracted back - MEOW!

GIVE ME A BREAK! ALL MY TEACHERS ARE REALLY OLD!

If you have a crush on your teachers you do everything to please them. If you have a crush on a pop star you buy all their records and put up posters of them.

It's all normal and it's all natural.

After a while things move on and you find a girlfriend or a different person to have a crush on.

what happens if you have a crush on a grape? it gives a little wine! boom.boom ... my name's J.C. goodnight.

You never grow out of crushes, but they get a little less intense and a little more fun as you get older.

Falling in love is the best thing that can happen to you.

And it **will** happen.

certainly is and it

There really is someone for every one in the world and everybody finds someone to fall in love with and be loved by.

happens to me almost every time I meet a babe!

So don't worry – just keep on looking, You'll find someone. It might not be for a while but almost everyone finds someone to love.

↳ SURELY NOT AS GOOD AS WINNING THE FA CUP?

IS THIS A PROMISE?

being
gay

First off, despite what you might think, it

isn't weird or
abnormal

to develop a huge crush on, or even be sexually attracted to, members of the same sex. It's just all part of your hormones playing havoc during puberty.

It's very common. **Does it make you gay?**
No it doesn't.

⇒ yeah. well I've got loads of girls crawling all over me. I just wanted to make that clear!

Sometimes people take crushes a little further and experiment physically with members of the same sex. again, there is nothing wrong with that. Lots of people experiment with their sexuality for a long time.

In fact, one out of every three boys and one out of every five girls have messed around with members of the same sex.

You freaked by that?
You shouldn't be. It's completely normal.

And just because you experiment it doesn't mean that you are gay.

LIKE THINKING THAT THE BOY SHEARER IS THE BEST!

SHEARER

Even if you did decide you preferred other blokes to girls, what's the problem with that? It's estimated that

ONE IN TEN
people in the UK are gay.

Just because you might find other lads sexually attractive it doesn't mean that you are weird, a pervert or have got to start wearing women's underwear.
Gay blokes are just the same as straight blokes.
They just fancy other men.

- They don't watch you in the shower.
- They don't try and sleep with every lad they talk to.
- They don't listen to nothing but Madonna.
- They don't cry at the drop of a hat.
- they don't all have unhealthy relationships with their mothers.

Gay men are all around you. They are teachers, pop stars, government officials, lawyers, policeman, comics, milk men. They are just the same as any other bloke.

No one should feel isolated or alone because of what they think their sexuality might be.

If you think you might be gay because you've got a crush on another bloke and that idea worries you, go and talk to someone about it.

- If you feel isolated, alone or confused because of the way you feel...
- If you don't think you can tell anyone – or that if you did your parents wouldn't understand...
- If you feel that you are the only gay bloke in the world...

GO AND TALK

= talking is good!

Your GP or the Gay Switchboard will both be able to offer sound advice.

blah blah blah blah blah

In the same way that finding yourself having a crush on another bloke doesn't mean that you are gay, dating a girl doesn't mean that you aren't gay.

IT'S HORSES FOR COURSES!

Some blokes have **always known** that they prefer blokes, some blokes try girls and **then decide** they prefer blokes, some blokes like both blokes and girls (*they're bisexual*), some settle down and get **married**, have children and **then realise** that they **prefer blokes**. There are no rules about how you feel or who you should fancy.

Everything is normal.

Always remember that sexuality isn't a switch that is either on or off, gay or straight. It's more like a slide that will eventually nestle somewhere between gay and straight, but may be closer to one than the other.

ON

OFF

making a relationship work

(BATTERIES NOT INCLUDED)

(also known as BEING ROMANTIC)

GIRLS HATE ALL THAT SWEETIE-PIE STUFF. ALL THEY WANT IS A PACKET OF CHIPS AND A QUICK SNOG!

WHY NOT

romance? that is easy - V.C. IS romance. I'm a lurve god!

Just because you've got off with a girl and asked her out it doesn't mean you can sit back on your heels and relax. The toughest challenge is yet to come.

You've got to make your relationship work out.

How do you do that?

Well, with something that lads of all ages find difficult, embarrassing and sometimes downright impossible. **It's called** *ROMANCE.*

(- NO WE DON'T)

IS THAT FLOWERS AND STUFF?

Romance is so very important because
when the romance goes, your whole relationship will
fall down round your ears. **It's true.**

*You can lust after someone, love them
so much you feel like you're floating,
but the day the romance dies is the day
the clock is counting down to the big
split between the two of you.*

So how do you capture the romance of a relationship
and keep it? Well here's a home truth – you meet
someone, you fall in love and

everything that girl says and does is romantic.

They can burp, fart or vomit and you'll
think it's cute, endearing and sweet. But
once you've got to know someone a little
bit more, that's when the romance begins
to disappear – when you know exactly
what your gorgeous girlfriend is about to
say, do or even think.

And that's when you've got to roll up
your sleeves and start working at romance
because if you don't nurture romance it
will kick its little legs in the air, roll over
and snuff it. And so will your relationship.

SIMPLE! WANT TO KEEP THE
ROMANCE? CUT OFF YOUR EARS.

No way! girls always lust after me – I'm just so cool.

YUK·!·
NO
WAY!

JL's top romance tips
1- snogging 2- holding hands 3- snogging
4- girls listening to me 5- snogging
6- listening to my jokes and laughing.

SO WHAT IS ROMANCE?

It's not just up to us lads to make romance work. The girls have to do their fair share – they just seem to find it a lot easier than guys.

So just what is romantic?

Anything.
Everything.

All the expected stuff – flowers, chocolates, love letters. That's all romantic.

But remember, if you are being romantic, keep it simple. A single flower can be just as romantic as a huge bunch of roses and a massive box of chocolates.

In fact, if you go too far overboard it can just all become very embarrassing and instead of being flattered or touched, your girlfriend will feel awkward and uncomfortable.

The key to real romance is to use your head. That's why a

bacon sandwich and a cup of tea in a plastic cup

at the right time, in the right place, with the right person, can be so much more romantic than a four course meal in a posh restaurant.

[handwritten annotations:]

ED'S LIST OF AWFUL PET NAMES 4 YOUR GIRL-FRIEND ⇓
1 - SNUGGLES
2 - TEDDY
3 - POOH POOH
4 - SAGGY BUM
5 - SCRUMMY

me →

with a signed photo

love J.C.

– I give all the girls I go out

USE MY HEAD!

OH - NO!

sandwich ←

{! tea

girl ←

that's so romantic J.C.

✱ very romantic!

✱ very cheap!

Romance is at its best when it's simple and when there has been some thought behind it.

Anyone, if they've got the cash, can take a girl to the cinema, buy her chocolates and then whisk her off to dinner.

That's not romance – that's just easy.

Romance is all about creating or giving something special to someone you love that only the two of you will understand.

That's why a plastic frog – *ribbit* – if your loved one is mad about plastic frogs – can be just as *romantic* as a diamond ring. – *my eyes shine like diamonds!*

What else is romantic?

Well it doesn't have to involve the giving of gifts. Just taking time to be with someone can be romantic. It's very easy when you've been with someone for a while to **take them for granted** – to forget just how special they are and how lucky you are to be with them. Telling someone just how much you love them is the most romantic thing.

Or just ask her down the bottle – how much more romantic do you want?

- Walking in the park
- Sitting on a beach in the middle of winter
- Telling stories
- Sharing jokes and secrets
- Just cuddling up and burying you face in her jumper for hours

can all be so very *ROMANTIC.*

BUT BE CAREFUL.

↘ but not as romantic as being with me!

Some guys get it all wrong and are romantic all the time. Do that and you'll probably end up being shown the door. No one can stand having someone giving them gifts, sending them letters or being lovey dovey all the time.

3

↖ THIS IS THE DOOR

It would drive you mad.

-pibble, dribble piny, pony

Romance should be thought about, rationed, made special – it's not something for everyday.

And giving someone a bunch of flowers or walking in the park won't save your relationship if it's already over. No matter how romantic you are – if you and your girlfriend are destined to walk away from each other, you're going to whatever...

J.L. © copyright

ROMANCE RULES – 1 EVERY DAY

→ Romance won't save a relationship,

but it can help to stop it from going pear-shaped to begin with. – *that's odd – pear-shaped is how I like*

Romance should be fun, exciting, tingly and wonderful. Romance is clichéd. It's all about hugs, flowers, sunsets, midnight walks and dancing in the kitchen. Romance is all about losing yourself in someone else. It's probably the best thing there is in the entire world and you can't be in love without it. And us guys really can do it – there aren't any big secrets to being romantic – **just use your imagination and keep it simple.**

my girl friends to be!

NO CHANCE OF A GOAL IN EXTRA TIME? :-)

getting intimate

←yes!!
getting it on!
doing the wild thing!
making out!

You've got past the date. You've got past becoming an item with your girlfriend. You've even fallen in love.

Getting intimate is just another obstacle to tackle.

It's natural: you're with someone who you think is pretty neat, they think you are pretty neat, so you want to explore and touch and cuddle them.

STRUTH!
I CAN COPE WITH A QUICK SNOG AND GROPE – WHY GET INVOLVED WITH ALL HER PROBLEMS.

I'm the expert!!

cool!
luuve
ooh
Julie

But it's important that you get intimate with someone for all the right reasons and not all the wrong ones.

So what are these reasons?

WRONG REASONS X

1. All your friends claim to have done it loads

They haven't – lads are terrible braggers. When you all get together you love to make up stories. You shouldn't, but you do.

Almost every bloke brags about his conquests and almost every bloke is making it all up. And besides, even if your best mate isn't making it up and has actually undone a girl's bra, that doesn't mean that you have to do the same as him. Take your time.

2. You took a girl to the pictures or bought her a pizza.

So you took someone out – it doesn't mean that she has to pay you back in kind. That's just ridiculous. If you think that, you really need to do some serious reconsidering. When a girl gives you a hug it's because she wants to, not because you bought her a present.

3. You tell someone that you love them

Intimacy and love are two different things. It's nice when they happen together – but they don't always, so don't get one and automatically expect the other.

HAVE YOU HEARD ABOUT THAT GIRL IN 4C ... WOW!

I can undo a girl's bra with one hand, in the dark. Ucs - magic fingers!

> but I don't even have to take girls out! they just phone me up all the time. SMUG

4. You've been dating for a given length of time
You can be with someone for years before you both feel
ready to commit to any kind of *physical love*. The
whole point about becoming intimate is that everyone
has to make their own rules. It's much better to wait
until you feel the time and the person is right.

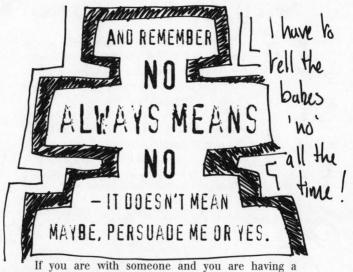

AND REMEMBER
NO
ALWAYS MEANS
NO
– IT DOESN'T MEAN
MAYBE, PERSUADE ME OR YES.

I have to tell the babes 'no' all the time!

If you are with someone and you are having a
snuggle on the sofa and they want to stop,

**YOU'VE GOT TO
STOP.**

And likewise if you want to stop,

**THEY'VE GOT TO
STOP.**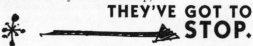

So what about the **right reasons**

Well – there is only one really right reason:

because you love someone and they love you.

You want to share something special and be close to someone. Get that right and a hug will make time stand still.

You might be tempted to take things further and go to bed with your love monster. But remember that straight sex is illegal if you are under 16 and gay sex is illegal if you are under 18.

DON'T BREAK THE LAW – IT'S THERE TO PROTECT YOU.

If you or your girlfriend are thinking about making some sort of physical commitment to each other, the most important thing is not sweet music, low lights or a romantic setting. The most important thing is to talk, so you both know what you want.

There is a huge pressure on lads to somehow prove that they are **real men** by getting intimate with as many girls as possible. But you really don't have to if you don't want to.

Getting intimate is great. **It's wonderful,** end of the world, lose yourself in someone, great.

you should see my little black book full of my ex's.

65

And that's pretty good. But if it's not with the right person, or you find yourself going further than you want to and feeling uncomfortable, it can also be lousy.

dumping

Let's start with,
dumping someone

You might have thought that it was tough plucking up the courage to ask a girl out, making your relationship public and telling her that you love her. But none of that is as tough as telling her that it's all over.

— sorry babe it just ain't working!

No one enjoys dumping.

No one likes to see someone upset and sad.

No one likes that look on a girl's face when you are about to tell them that it's all over, and they know what's coming, but everything in their eyes is begging you not to say it.

Vic's top dumping lines

1- there's the door - you know how to use it

2- you're history - no good to me

That's a horrible moment.
But sometimes it's the

only thing to do.

You can be with someone and love them loads, they can make you laugh and be your best friend – but if it's time to say,

3- I prefer your sister

'I'M SORRY, IT'S ALL OVER,'

then it's time to move on.

4- I love you too much

5- You're just not cool - get with the programme.

Dumping is easy – just don't phone!!

66

Sometimes things just don't work out.
- It's nobody's fault.
- It's not something that can be avoided.
- It just happens.

it wasn't me!

A wise man once said
" we might not be able to tell the moment when love begins, but we always know the exact moment it ends."

I never have any regrets.

Love them and leave them.

And that is so true.

You can't help falling in love and you can't help falling out of love. But when you do want to split it's best to be honest, face up to your emotions and respect your ex enough to let them know how you feel.

The law according to J.C

I JUST T MY MATES TELL TUE GIRL

So the question is,

is there a right or wrong way to split up with someone?

And the answer is not really. But as a basic rule there are some things that work when you dump someone and some things that don't.

THAT'S ME

*GOLDEN DUMPING RULE:
BE HONEST AND BE STRONG.*

thats me

Telling someone you have been close to that it's all over is never going to be easy. It's a rough ride and it can be just as bad for the person who is doing the dumping as the person who is being dumped. But no matter how much it hurts you, or your ex, when you dump someone you have to simply **decide what you want to do** and **do it.**

OH ER - NRD!!

GIGGLE GIGGLE!

And that's when you have to be **STRONG.**

The dumped girl will

HATE YOUR GUTS

this is what usualy happens

plewz . plewz . plewz . plewz . plewz . go out with me again.

if you tell them it's all over and then let yourself be talked into trying to *make it all work out*, only to realise after a while that you never wanted to try and give things a second go to begin with.

It's tough when you are faced with someone who is very upset, someone you care about. It is very tempting to say you're sorry and that you've changed your mind and, 'Yes – I'd like to try and make things work out.'

DON'T BOTHER.

HEY, ONCE THE BABE HAS BLOWN IM BACK WITH MY MATES!

I guess.

err...ok...

It's statistically proven that most couples who get to the point of splitting up only to try and make things work out don't succeed. They end up going their separate ways and there is even more **heart- ache** and **pain** when they finally do break up.

REMEMBER:

9OOD ADVICE.

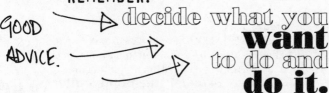

decide what you **want** to do and **do it.**

Unfortunately when you split up with someone it's a time for you to be a little selfish. I'M A LITTLE SMELL FISH!!

If **YOU** are unhappy in a relationship **YOU** have to leave it.

If that means your ex is going to be upset, cry and be heart broken, that's a real shame – and that should upset you as much as it upsets them. But ultimately it's true that

I have to keep telling all my girls this.

no girl wants to be with a boy if he isn't happy about being with her.

So by being true to your own feelings you are doing the right thing by your girlfriend, although she might not see it that way at the time. Always remember that you are leaving someone because you want to and

NEVER USE THE LINE,

'I'm doing this for your own good,'

→ hey- that's one of my best lines!

69

OK IF THERE IS A GOOD FOR THE HATCH ON!

because **YOU'RE NOT**, and it's very patronising.

When you do finally tell someone it's all over be truthful about why you want to split up – but don't be nasty.

If there isn't a set reason, you just feel that things aren't working out – say that. That's good enough in itself.

I ALWAYS LISTEN TO HER – BUT I STILL DO WHAT I WANT!!

LISTEN to what your girlfriend has to say about splitting up and listen to how she feels about it – but don't be talked out of splitting unless you are 100%, **24 carat, diamond cutter certain** you want to be.

And once you've dumped someone **don't, don't, don't** get off with them next time you're at a party together.

by splitting up!

Do, and there will be lots of anger and bitterness.

Make your decision, be sure it's what you want and live by it.

But it isn't always going to be that easy and all too often you can find yourself wimping out and making some of the classic all time dumping mistakes. So here are a few guidelines for dumping...

WHO ARE YOU CALLING A WIMP??

FROM A GREAT HEIGHT?

→1. **Where to dump**

Pick the place carefully. **Think about it.** Striding up to your girlfriend at a club where she is surrounded by all her mates and saying,

← this happens all the time!

'Sorry babe it's all over, I'm going out with your best friend,'

and then proceeding to **snog** said **best friend** is pretty bad. Picking a place when you know you can be alone in private and then telling her, so if she wants to cry and get upset she can (and, importantly, so can you) is much better.

THE OLD DUMP AND RUN?

A good place is their house, especially if you know that they are going to be there on their own. You'll have somewhere that is private so there can be tears and talk, but it's also somewhere that you can leave when the time comes.

Things can get a little embarrassing if you dump someone at your house and then they refuse to leave until you take it all back.

V.C's biggest problem

2. **When to dump**

Pick your moment. You owe someone that much.

Don't dump them just before they go on holiday, first thing in the morning at school or just before exams start.

A good time is a Saturday afternoon – both you and she will have the weekend to start getting over it and

I'm not leaving until you tell me that you love me again..

→ THE BEST DUMPING TIME IS JUST BEFORE THE BIG MATCH.

there should be friends around, or at least on the other end of a phone, to lend support.

3. How to dump — *Just don't phone — they get the message!*

You **DON'T** want to do the dumping **over the phone,** by letter or in public. That's **tacky** and shows a lack of respect for the person you are splitting up with. You should always dump someone to their face – you owe them that – which means you

NEVER, EVER, EVER GET YOUR FRIEND TO DUMP SOMEONE FOR YOU.

WHY NOT? *IT'S EASY*

And dont

dump and run.

If you are splitting up with someone you owe them their right to be upset. You have to face them and their tears. *↳ if a babe turns on the water works I'm out of the door!*

72

And one of the biggest

NO-NOS

as far as dumping someone goes is to take the easy
way out and

get off with another girl
behind their backs.

what? but that's the most fun!

That's pretty cheap and nasty.

Why?

Because you are using the person you are getting off
with to get you out of your relationship with your
girlfriend, your girlfriend is going to be really hurt and
it shows that you just don't care enough to face her and
talk things through.

If you do leave someone because you've met
someone else that's fine, it happens all the time.

But it shows a

huge

lack of respect for yourself and your current girlfriend if
you don't finish one thing before you start another.

Also it's **not fair** to make your girlfriend's life so
unpleasant that she **dumps you**. If you want to get
out of the relationship it's up to you to get out of it.

Don't be nasty to her in front of your friends,
never phone her,
or pretend that she doesn't exist,
in the hopes that she'll get the message.

THAT'S THE COWARD'S WAY OUT.

4. What to say ➡️

DON'T:

— what's wrong with 'hey babe take a hike?'

- Say anything hurtful:
  '*You're too immature for me.*'
  '*You were just a phase.*'
  '*I only went out with you because I felt sorry for you.*'

- Say anything naff:
  '*You're too good for me.*'
  '*I'll always love you.*'
  '*I'll be your friend until the day I die.*'

these are all my lines! the thing is — sometimes it's easier to be cheesy!

- Say anything untrue:
  '*I'll never love anyone else.*'
  '*It's the best for both of us.*'
  '*No, of course I'm not going out with your best friend*'

DO:

- Be clear and definite:
  '*This really is what I want. I'm sorry if that hurts you, but I think it's the best.*'

HOW ABOUT TAKING OUT AN ADVERT IN THE PAPERS?!?

- *Be kind:*
  'I've had a great time with you and
  it would be great if we could stay
  friends although I understand you
  might not want that.'

So that's how to dump – but what if you have been dumped?

getting dumped

let's get one thing straight – no-one ever dumps me!

GETTING DUMPED HURTS MORE THAN ANYTHING ELSE IN THE WORLD.

IT DOESN'T HURT ME – IN A REAL BLOKE

Having your girlfriend turn to you one day and say,

'I don't think we should see each other anymore,' – *like a girl is going to say that*

can make your entire world turn into an angry, bitter ball of tears and sadness.

to me!

GETTING DUMPED IS HORRIBLE.
IT'S THE END OF THE WORLD.

You've had the carpet pulled out from under you.
The sky is falling on your head.
You want to curl up into a ball and be left alone forever.

You have every right to be upset, confused and sad.

You don't have a right to make your ex's life hell with phone calls at all hours, unexpected visits and letters begging for you to get back together.

It's so untrue that if you get dumped by someone you can somehow win them back with flowers, poetry or persistence.

You can't,

it's been decided, it's over.

⟹ what's the point trying to win her back— just get off with her best mate!

It's going to hurt.

It's going to feel like there is nothing you can do to make yourself whole again. You are going to want to see your ex at every opportunity you get – and then hate her every time you do see her. It's a time for you to cry, to mourn the passing of a big love, to grieve and then to move on.

hello babe

— hello J.C...
giggle.

IT ISN'T
WORTH
FALLING IN
LOVE IF YOU

JUST END UP
GETTING HURT -

JUST STICK WITH
FOOTIE!

It's one of the toughest times a bloke ever has to face and it's a time for courage.

And ~~don't think~~ just because you are a bloke that you aren't allowed to get upset when someone ~~dumps~~ you.

Don't think that you have to grin and bear it, take it on the chin or shrug it off.

You are allowed to cry, you are allowed to be upset, and you are allowed to feel like someone has ripped out your still beating heart and jumped up and down on it.

You feel sad – let it all out.

Cry. Blub. Sniffle.

he, he, he

ex-girl friend ⟶

It's the best thing for you, because then you can try and start getting over someone. If you don't let out the tears and anger and hurt then you'll never be able to respect the girl's wishes and respect yourself enough to accept that it

squished heart ↑

really is
over. ...the top.

THIS IS
WHAT THEY'LL
DO TO YOU!!

BETTER OFF WITHOUT
THEM!

There is no point trying to deny it, refusing to accept it or trying to change it. Cry, watch soppy movies, listen to your favourite records, do anything to get rid of that

GNAWING EMPTINESS
THAT YOU FEEL INSIDE

– because it will go.
It might not feel like it at the time,
but it will.

I'M A GNAWING EMPTINESS

No one is ever ready to be **HEART-BROKEN** and no one wants to be a **HEART-BREAKER**.

Dumping, and being dumped, are the risks we all take when we fall in love, but if we didn't take those risks, we'd never find that special someone, and it's so worth it when you finally find someone that means the world to you.

getting over it

Mending a broken heart isn't an easy thing to do.

→ LIKE TAKING A PENALTY?

There aren't any **instant**, **just add water** cures that allow a bloke to mend his feelings, control his emotions and get on with his life.

a broken heart

this is what all those girls hearts look like.

↗ *A PATCH*

Hearts don't come with stick-on patches, they can't be mended with spit and sellotape and no matter how much we try and pretend that everything is fine - it usually isn't.

TICK TOCK TICK TOCK

THE ONLY THING THAT WILL MEND A BROKEN HEART IS TIME.

* *AND A HOME WIN!*

* *and a snog from another girl*

If you've just been dumped – or if you've just dumped someone – it takes time to get over it. You will probably want to be by yourself a lot, to cry and to feel blue,

which is all <u>FINE</u> and <u>NORMAL</u>.

Some days you wake up and you'll think things are hopeless, you'll never fall in love again and you'll be unhappy for the rest of your life.

not me!. – give me five

But it does get better.

minutes and I'd be back on the pull!

|| Slowly, and painfully, hearts mend.

Just don't expect it to happen overnight.

YER, YER LARDY - DAR

GIRLS' STUFF!!

79

It's a rule of thumb that when someone dumps you it takes twice as long to get over it as you went out with them for.

Seen someone for **six months**?
It will probably take **about a year.**

You won't be sad for that amount of time and you won't mope around and be depressed. You'll probably get together with other girls, maybe even have another long term relationship. But to be

TOTALLY

COMPLETELY,

'I'm fine about this, I really am,'

over someone can take a **long, long time**. Longer than most people realise.

And don't expect to stop loving someone just because you've been dumped. A broken heart isn't cured by trying to forget that you once really cared for someone and it isn't about hating them. — I love all my ex's...

When you really and truly fall in love with a girl – no matter what happens – there will always be a part of you in fact that will continue to care for her. That's normal and I love rather nice because it means that you never forget that all person or the special time you had together. ladies!

And before you stop reading and turn back to the pages with the **mucky stuff** on it –

I ALWAYS REMEMBER MY
SPECIAL TIMES WITH GIRLS!
NUDGE – NUDGE – WINK – WINK

THE SAME THING HAPPENED TO ME WHEN MY TEAM MISSED OUT ON THE CUP – I WAS GUTTED FOR AGES!

BOYS BEHAVING BADLY AROUND GIRLS

THIS IS IMPORTANT.

You fell in love.
It didn't work.
You split up.

Don't try and substitute HATE for LOVE.

It's always better to remember the good times rather than the bad.
In fact it will make you happier in the long term.

Honest – it will.

And another thing: you don't mend a broken heart by jumping from one girlfriend to another. It's tempting. You feel low, you feel sad, you feel like you want a shoulder to cry on. A lot of guys do it. They split up with a girl, or a girl dumps them, and within days – maybe even hours – they're in another relationship.

but there are so many girls and so little time!

Unfortunately it rarely works out.

81

You can't substitute one thing for another and

you can't substitute one person for another.

EXCEPT IN FOOTBALL

You've got to give yourself time to get over one relationship before you move on to the next. If you don't give yourself enough time you'll end up leap frogging from one unhappy relationship to another, because it's a fact that if you start seeing someone when you are on the rebound, it doesn't last.

Falling in love and getting over being in love isn't an exact science. Different things work for different people – but no matter how you go about patching up your heart, dusting yourself down and finding someone else to love, it's always best to give yourself time.

CLICHÉ ALERT, but...

I've never been heart broken.

time is a great healer

It's probably a cliché because it's true.

Now before this book turns into a soppy Mills and Boon romance let's move on to the next chapter which talks, amongst other things, about the old five fingered shuffle...yep, wanking.

Broken a few hearts – but never heart broken.

LOSER!

– IM ON THE REBOUND!

CHAPTER TWO

BOYS' BODIES BEHAVING BADLY

You hit puberty like an

EXPRESS TRAIN HEADING STRAIGHT FOR HORMONESVILLE

and all kinds of things begin to happen. *Maybe for some – but it was easy for me!*

Both your body and mind change and sometimes it's difficult to keep track of all the

weird,

wacky

and wonderful

things that are happening to you.

We deal with the mind stuff in the next chapter. This one is all about bodies.

Puberty for boys starts and stops any time between

Do you get a membership card?

10 and **18**.

It's completely normal and it doesn't make the slightest difference whether you are an early or late member of the puberty club – the changes will be the same.

Let's kick off with

bad teenage moustaches

cool!

cool!

aka facial hair.

FACIAL HAIR

They start to grow, but not overnight. Don't expect to go to bed with no hair on your face and wake up the next day looking like Father Christmas. *– ho, ho, ho - fancy a present girls?*

To begin with the hair is soft and probably only on the upper lip and maybe on the chin. But over a couple of years the hair gets thicker and more wiry and spreads all over your cheeks, chin and upper lip.

And as for **when** you start to shave – well that's up to you.

HOWEVER, IT'S PROBABLY BEST AT LEAST TO HAVE SOMETHING THERE TO SHAVE OFF.

Boy- do I need a shave!

IF YOU START TO SHAVE TOO EARLY YOU ONLY AGGRAVATE THE SKIN AND GIVE YOURSELF A NASTY RASH.

EXCELLENT... JOIN THE DOTS!

now that is a nasty rash.

It's also entirely up to you whether you

wet shave

using a razor and shaving soap or foam, or

dry shave

with an electric shaver.

Most lads start out wet shaving because it's quicker and probably easier if you haven't got that much to shave off.

So what do you need?

— a fast car

— a pretty girlfriend

— lots of cash

— new shades.

Well, for your first shave you will need:

- **Some facial hair.**
- **A razor.**
  A disposable one is fine, but one of the more expensive models with a swivel head will give you a more comfortable shave.
- **Some shaving foam.**
  This usually comes in a can, although it is still possible to get hold of the old-fashioned cakes of shaving soap.
- **A mirror.** Obviously.
- **Some hot water.**
- **Some moisturiser.**
  If you haven't got any, you could always pinch some of your mum's or sister's.

GET TO THE HEP BEAT CRAZY CAT!

ISN'T THAT WHAT GIRLS USE?

U.G's list of silly beards

1- Farther Christmas
2- Jazz man goatees
3- country and western singer beards
4- Merlin and all other wizards
5- Shaggy from Scooby Doo.

86

And how do you go about it?

Run some hot, but not scalding, water and wash your face with normal soap. This softens the bristles and makes them easier to cut.

- **Squirt a small amount of shaving foam into your hand, lather it up and rub into your beard.** Or lack of it. The idea with the foam is to reduce the friction between your face and the razor and to soften up the hair even more.

– cool!

- **Run your razor under some hot water and then begin to shave.** Always shave downwards and with the growth of the beard. Start with the cheeks and then work round the upper lip leaving the chin until last – that's where the toughest hairs grow.

- **Rinse your razor often, either under hot water or in the sink, making sure that the blades aren't becoming clogged with hair.**

- **Once you've finished, rinse off any remaining shaving foam with warm water and check for missed patches.** If you've missed a bit you can run the razor quickly over that particular patch.

smooth as a baby's bum! (but less smelly.)

I HAVEN'T MISSED ANY!

- **If you're clear, rinse your face with cold water.** This helps to close up the pores and seal the skin. Don't splash on loads of aftershave. Aftershave uses alcohol as its base and that's why when you put it on after shaving it stings. It's much better to pat your face dry, checking behind the ears for any stray foam and then use a little moisturiser to give your face back its softness and flexibility.

WELL — I THINK IT'S FOR GIRLS — :(

USING MOISTURISER DOESN'T MAKE YOU A BIG GIRL'S BLOUSE. IT'S VERY GOOD FOR YOU AND PROTECTS YOUR SKIN.

- After shaving it's always best to rinse your razor thoroughly under
  very hot water,
  making sure you get rid of any clogged hairs.

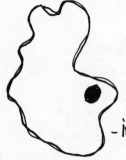

- You should probably **change** the head of **your razor** once every **two or three shaves** – leave it any longer than that and the blades will get blunt and they won't cut as well. They'll also become a breeding ground for germs and bacteria. Not nice.

- IM A BACTERIA.

• If you **cut** yourself while shaving, don't stick on a little bit of toilet paper. That will do nothing for you and as soon as you take the paper off, you'll start to **bleed** again.

It's better to let the skin close up of its own accord. If you want you could swab a cut with TCP, but it shouldn't be that deep and will be fine if you just leave it alone.

what do you mean – 'have I cut myself?'

Now, if you suffer from particularly **bad spots or acne** then shaving can be something of a

nightmare.

If it's just the occasional eruption you can probably steer your razor round it, but if you are suffering from a really bad attack you can try one of two things:

1. ## Grow a beard

(which is not only not allowed in a lot of schools but also makes you look like a Wild West frontiers man – fine in the wild west, less fine in Guildford), or

– YEE-ARR!

THE RAZOR AND ZIT SLALOM – IT'S A NEW OLYMPIC SPORT = HONEST

89

2. <u>Use</u> <u>an</u> <u>electric</u> <u>razor.</u>

Why? Well, if you dry shave with electric shavers your skin won't be agitated by the use of shaving foam.

A **decent** electric razor can be bought for about £20 and will be gentler on the skin. If you want to try using one, it's probably best to go for a **MULTI-HEADED RAZOR** with three small metal foils that make a triangle on the shaving

like this!

face. The other main type of electric razor has one single, long foil. This is fine too, but the three-headed versions give you more control over a

LIKE THIS!

bumpy surface.

nt zit-prone to eruptions

Just like with a wet shaver, you have to clean the shaving heads after every shave to **stop** the build up of **hair**, **skin** and **bacteria**. *-he.he.he its all my fault!*

Which brings us to:

spots, zits, eruptions...

otherwise knows as **A C N E**

Almost everybody gets the occasional zit during puberty
– but unfortunately some people get them worse than
others. What can you do?

Unfortunately
very little.

• Spots are caused by
pores in your skin
becoming blocked
by **EXCESS OILS**...

*so I get the occasional
spot - lim
still
cool!*

...that have been
released because
of the **HORMONE**
RIOT going on in
your body...

...that in turn
has been caused
by **PUBERTY**.

*(SO I GET THE OCCASIONAL
SPOT - SO WHAT ?*

And you don't just get them on your face.
They can also appear on your
back and *shoulders*
and, to a lesser extent,
on your *chest*.

*it's the human
dot to dot book!*

91

So what can be done about these

pesky red, pus-filled monsters?

- he, he, he I'm a puss filled monster and I'm out to get you!

The most important thing is to

WASH REGULARLY

with a non-scented soap.

You can try using a **MEDICATED** soap or one of the many anti-spot creams, pastes and applications that you can buy from the chemists, but they will probably do little good.

rip off

Normal soap and water is just as effective as any scientifically tested, new improved, breakthrough.

If your spots get particularly bad you should get yourself along to your doctor who can prescribe **drugs** to reduce the puffiness and swelling.

- NEW
ZIT ✱
AWAY
SCIENTIFICALLY PROVEN - VERY EXPENSIVE - BUY ME - GET A GIRL - BUY ME.

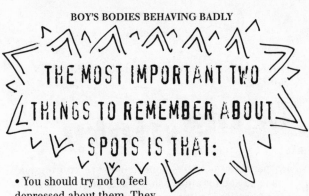

THE MOST IMPORTANT TWO THINGS TO REMEMBER ABOUT SPOTS IS THAT:

• You should try not to feel depressed about them. They usually go away eventually and leave you with a smooth complexion and,

• You mustn't scratch, pick or pop them. The temptation can be almost overwhelming to squeeze those zits. But don't. If you do you might end up with scarring.

Greasy hair

The same greasiness and excess oils that cause spots can also give you particularly greasy hair. Again, wash your hair often and thoroughly and you should be able to keep the

gloopiness

down to a minimum.

Don't forget that during puberty, while your body is changing, your hormones will be in *full on party mode.* That's why you get spots and greasy hair.

HORMONES HAVING A PARTY

- GREAT PARTY! DO YOU COME HERE OFTEN?

- ALL THE TIME. FANCY A DANCE?

93

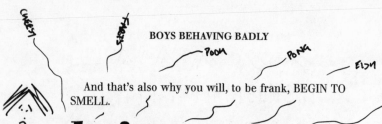

CHEESE

YUCK

POOH

PONK

FISH

And that's also why you will, to be frank, BEGIN TO SMELL.

BUT GIRLS
LIKE THAT
MANLY
SMELL!

being *stinky*

It's perfectly normal – your glands are growing and changing and for a while they will produce particularly strong-smelling sweat. It's nothing to be ashamed of – but it is a good idea to get under the

shower, or into a **hot bath**, and have a

good scrub down

regularly.

You are going to get especially whiffy under your arms and round your penis and scrotum and on your feet.

So wash them.

Regularly.

SURELY
NOT

EVERY

DAY

‖ Every day.

And don't forget to change your shirt.

There is **no point** getting yourself smelling sweet as a daisy only to put a **stinky** shirt back on.

DON'T KNOW HOW TO CLEAN A SHIRT?

IT'S VERY SIMPLE.

1. **Stinky shirt.**
2. **Washing machine.**

WHAT'S THIS?
OH IT'S ONE OF THOSE
WASHING THINGS – FOR MUM

NEVER IRON MY SHIRTS - IT I RARELY WASH THEM EITHER.

3. Washing powder.
4. Put shirt in machine and turn it on.
5. Dry shirt.
5a. Iron shirt (optional).
6. Wear clean shirt.

Notice that at **NO POINT** in that list are the words, wait for *mum, sister, dad* or anyone else to wash shirt for you.

AND BESIDES ITS A LITTLE KNOWN FACT THAT AFTER 6 MONTHS THEY STOP SMELLING!

There is nothing worse

than body odour, or $\mathbb{BO}$, but sometimes it just can't be helped.

↑ stinky!

I shower all the time - everything about me smells like flowers.

ALL YOU CAN DO IS SHOWER OR BATH EVERY DAY AND USE A GOOD, STRONG, DEODORANT.

Whether you use a **spray** or
roll-on deodorant
is up to you, but if you use a spray it's less likely to block the pores under your arms and cause an infection – something that can happen with roll-ons.

95

You can also use an aftershave and splash it all over your body to help hide any smells.

But AFTERSHAVE ISN'T A SUBSTITUTE for washing and remember that a little goes a long way.

A quick splash on your chest will cover up a multitude of ~~whiffy nasties~~ that might develop after you've had a good wash with plenty of **hot water** and **soap**.

But **too much**

will make you smell like the perfume counter at Boots,

which is just as bad.

So what about the other changes that happen to your body during puberty?

Voices

How come you can be talking to someone and have a shrill voice one second and then after a bit of a

WoBbLe,

a deep **booming** voice the next?

Well it's to do with the Adam's apple which is not a new and exciting form of fruit, but the part of your body that's just below your chin, sticks out a bit and hurts like hell if you ever get punched on it.

I HAD A VERY LOW VOICE SINCE BIRTH — BECAUSE IM THAT MUCH OF A MAN!

GRRRRR

— IM AN ADAMS APPLE! NOT.

rubbish — I've got some of the very best aftershaves around. The have you use — the better — girls love you to smell good!

(ie what is that stink?)

It's job is to be in charge of the change in a lad's voice.

If you get a little **EXCITED** when your voice first starts to break, it will all of a sudden sound like you've been **sucking a helium balloon.**

This is nothing to worry about and it will settle down given a little time and find it's natural, deeper pitch.

How **l o n g** will it take?

Well, that's impossible to say. For some lads your voice can take months to break completely, for others it can happen over a couple of weeks.

body hair

I'm afraid if you are expecting to go from **smoothly smooth** to a **walking carpet** in a matter of days then you've got another think coming.

It's perfectly normal for body hair to develop at different times on different parts of your body, so if you've got hairy legs don't expect to have a chest rug at the same time.

IT'S WEIRD BUT SOME GUYS REALLY ARE HAIRIER THAN OTHERS.

LIKE THE YETI - NOW THAT IS WEIRD!

But don't think just because you've got a little bit more chest hair that it makes you more of a man – it doesn't.

And despite what you might have heard – it's not unusual to have hairs growing on your back and on your bum cheeks.

A HAIRY BUM! WELL, GUESS IT STOPS YOU GETTING COLD!

– all the girls go wild about all my body hair!!

97

Some girls make a big thing about not liking hairy backs and bums. **BUT DON'T WORRY ABOUT IT** – unless you look in a mirror you're not going to be able to see them and if a girl gets to the stage where she sees your back or your bum, hopefully she'll have other things on her mind.

indeed!!!
ladies!!
hell-o!!

You'll also notice hair in that whole area below the belt. A mass of thick wiry hairs, called pubic hair or pubes, start to grow.

Again, no two guys are exactly the same, so if you are in the shower after footie and you cast a quick eye round the **pride** and **joy** of the first eleven you are going to see different sized and shaped willies and different amounts of pubic hair.

And by the way, you don't need to cut pubic hair.

It reaches a certain length and then stops. You don't need to pop down to the local barber and ask for a short, back and sides and a genital trim. But if you do have to shave your pubes, maybe because of an operation, they will grow back. They're clever like that.

So let's get down to your:

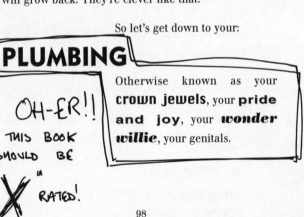

PLUMBING

Otherwise known as your **crown jewels**, your **pride and joy**, your *wonder willie*, your genitals.

SWEAT, BACK AND SIDES PLEASE – AND WHAT YOU'RE CUTTING.

OH-ER!!

THIS BOOK SHOULD BE "X" RATED!

98

Boys have the bodily equivalent of the Bermuda Triangle that covers the entire area of their genitals. And all through puberty things seem to appear and disappear in this area for what seems like no reason at all, although hopefully no ships or aircraft will go missing inside your boxers.

So what actually happens?

For a start a boy's testicles and penis get **bigger**.

How big?

Well how long is a piece of string? ⟹

a piece of string is this long - well at least mine is!

It varies, but not as much as you might think. Before puberty a boy's willy is about **3** to **5** cm when soft. After puberty it's about **6** to **10** cm when soft and **12** to **16** cm when **HARD**.

OK- BUT HAVE YOU GOT A RULER I COULD BORROW LATER?

Now before all you guys go running off with a ruler, no two guys are the same. And

SIZE MAKES NO DIFFERENCE AS TO HOW WELL IT WORKS.

And if you are wondering whether

the way you hang

is the same as the way every other lad hangs, it is more or less. You'd be surprised just how similar all willies are. Sure, no *two* are the same – but they all follow the # BASIC DESIGN.

– IS IT A COPYRIGHTED DESIGN.
– DOES IT HAVE A MAKER'S MARK?

Yours might curve off to the side a little or even curve up a little. **THAT'S PERFECTLY NORMAL.** Some guys have circumcised willies which means that they have had an operation at some point in their lives to pull back their foreskin, which is the piece of soft skin that covers the head of your penis, permanently. **It doesn't affect the way it works or what it feels like to be the proud owner of one.**

LIKE THIS

And some lads only have **one** testicle instead of the more usual **two**. They're either born that way, or have had one removed for medical reasons. If you only have **one** ball it doesn't affect how it works, what it feels like or whether you will be able to become a dad.

I wonder if anyone has ever had 3?

SO MOST PENIS AND TESTICLE SETS ARE MORE-OR-LESS THE SAME – AND THEY ALL DO THE SAME THINGS.

When you hit puberty, all of a sudden things in the trouser department start doing stuff

<u>all by themselves.</u>

You can be standing in a bus queue or waiting in line for school dinners and all of a sudden...

hello!

And as for first thing in the morning...not all lads join the scouts – but when they wake up,

all lads can make a tent

with their natural equipment and the duvet.

We are talking

like what? Playing the piano, doing my chemistry homework - now that would be useful!

BUT WHERE DO YOU GET THE PEGS FROM?

erections,

hard ons,

boners.

They come and go without any rhyme or reason.

BUT DON'T PANIC.

that's a shame. X-RAY vision would be quite fun - especially

Just because you get a hard on in public it doesn't mean that everyone can see. Only Superman has X-ray vision.
It might feel like it's sticking out like a flag pole, it might feel like you can't walk or that you've got an extra leg,

when the girls are playing net ball!

but it isn't that noticeable.

And now you've got this thing **looking up at** you at every turn, what are you going to do with it?

You want to **explore** it.

You want to **poke** and **prod** it, to – let's be frank – masturbate.

HELLO...
HELLO...
TALK TO
ME... IM
HERE...
HELLO!

Masturbation

otherwise know as,

*tossing off, **stroking**, wanking, **pulling the ploughman**, doing the five finger shuffle, **rubbing ronny**, spanking the monkey, **beating the meat**, strumming, **self manipulation**, self love, **exercising the bishop**, jerking off and **wristing**...*

to name but a few.

OH ER MRS!

THIS D

JUST SO

RUDE!!

  Some people think masturbation is a dirty thing to do – but it isn't and despite what you might have heard, everyone does it.

Everyone.

And you know what? There is nothing wrong with it. It's fun and it feels nice, otherwise people wouldn't be doing it in the first place.

So let's clear up a few of the stupid myths and old wives' tails that surround masturbation.

I used to until I discovered girls!

* IT WON'T MAKE YOU GO MAD OR BLIND.

* IT WON'T MAKE HAIR GROW ON YOUR PALMS.

* IT WON'T MAKE YOUR PENIS FALL OFF.

IT WON'T GIVE YOU SPOTS. *

IT WON'T T MAKE YOU INFERTILE. *

IT WON'T MAKE YOU A PERVERT. *

IT WON'T AFFECT YOUR ABILITY TO HAVE SEX IN THE FUTURE. *

[handwritten annotation: I'M GLAD THIS IS ALL TRUE — OTHERWISE I'D BE IN REAL TROUBLE!]

Now it's sometimes thought that masturbation is wrong or a sin, which is fine if that's what some people want to think, but always remember

it's what you *think* and *feel* that matters.

Never let anyone make you feel guilty for doing something that is perfectly natural.

What every sex expert agrees is that **masturbation** is the best way to discover things about your body and how you like to be touched. It's a way of exploring and discovering things about yourself and there is

absolutely nothing wrong with it.

Masturbating once, twice, even three times a month, *Nwuew!* a week, a day, an hour... that's all perfectly natural and perfectly fine.

As a very great man once said, *Woody Allen said that!*

nobody should knock masturbation - after all it's sex with someone you love.

VERY TRUE

Masturbation Time Out
Ok so it's normal. Everyone does it.
But what do you actually do?

Well, the dictionary definition of masturbation is the stimulation of the genitals by oneself until one reaches a sexual climax.

What?

In English that means you touch and stroke your penis, usually back and forth and up and down until you reach an

orgasm.

A **warm**, tingly **sensation** will start building round your penis and you will probably begin to **stroke faster** and faster.

You might start thinking **sexy thoughts** about girls, your geography teacher or a favourite pop star. The **tingly sensation grows and spreads** around your body until it reaches a **climax** that almost hurts. But it's a nice type of hurt, **like a big sneeze.**

That's when you **come** and **white sticky stuff**, your semen, **spurts out** of the end of your penis. And it feels **really nice.**

That's masturbating. And one very, **very** important point:

you never, ever run out of semen.

You could **masturbate** every day, all day, for hours on end and all you would end up with is a **tired wrist** and a **sore penis.**

No bloke has got a limited supply of spunk – your testicles make it on demand. Don't worry – you won't run out.

It's not just masturbating that involves **you, your best friend and a sticky mess.**

You might also have...

Handwritten annotations:

I dont know why you're telling me all of this. I've known this since I was ...

THAT'S GOOD TO KNOW

← SPUNK-O-METER.

THE "BEST FRIEND" YOU KEEP IN YOUR PANTS!

105

wet dreams.

What's a wet dream?

Well it's a dream, usually – but not always – about sex that results in a boy having an **orgasm in his sleep**. You wake up in the morning and you'll find a sticky patch on your sheets. There is nothing to be embarrassed about. Everyone has had one and you couldn't stop yourself even if you wanted to, because it's your body doing what's natural.

IM A STICKY PATCH.

Lads grow out of wet dreams – but **no one** ever grows out of masturbation.

← I grew out of them when I was 9

→ EVER. ←

So these are your body changes and what you can expect from them.

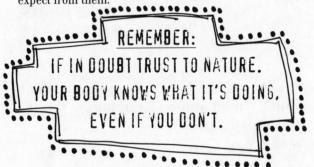

REMEMBER:
IF IN DOUBT TRUST TO NATURE.
YOUR BODY KNOWS WHAT IT'S DOING,
EVEN IF YOU DON'T.

OH-ER MRS!

Sexy thoughts

While you are getting into some heavy wrist action you might think sexy thoughts. That's fine too – it's called

fantasising

and everyone does it.

PLEASE...
NOT
MY
MATHS
TEACHER...
Yuk!

Just because you might have sexy thoughts about your **maths teacher** dressed as a **large rabbit** jumping up and down on a **trampoline** it doesn't mean that you want it to happen. When you have sexy thoughts you are just imagining them; you don't necessarily actually want them to happen. You should

NEVER FEEL GUILTY

about what you think about when you masturbate. Whatever it is, it's normal – just don't expect it to come true.

MAGAZINES

COOL DUDE WEEKLY
+ SHADES WEARING MONTHLY
are the only two I buy

Now you might get a little tired of just thinking about girls and want to start looking at some instead – some with few or no clothes on. You might start being distracted every time you go into your local newsagent by magazines – either fashion magazines that have girls dressed in **see-through tops** or maybe the ones on the top shelf. You know – the ones with titles like

Razzle, Naughty Neighbours and

Big and Bouncy.

STRUTH!!

GIGGLE, GIGGLE!

You might even want to buy one. That's fine – although a newsagent shouldn't sell you a porn magazine if you are **under 18**.

Just because you buy
Nude Girls in Jelly, *– that's the mag for me!*

or sneak a peek at the underwear section of your mum's mail order catalogue, it doesn't make you a pervert. Hundreds of thousands of men and even some women regularly buy and enjoy pornography. After all, porn has been around for thousands of years.

WHERE WOULD I SEE THESE MOSAICS AGAIN?

If you think that the contents of girly magazines is a bit saucy you should see some ancient Roman mosaics and statues.

NOW THEY WOULD MAKE YOUR EYES POP OUT.

But if you have bought your copy of Big And Bouncy and got it home there are some important things to remember. *U's top babes*

❶ All models in general,
and models in pornography in particular,
*1 – any
2 – any
3 – any*

aren't average women.

They're probably taller, slimmer and with **bigger breasts** than anyone else you know. And the same goes for movie stars and pop stars. They are *glamorous, beautiful and sexy*. That's part of why they do what they do – because their bodies are considered to be either perfect or sexy.

So don't expect your girlfriend to measure up to the girl on the centre spread of Playboy.

YOUR GIRLFRIEND WON'T HAVE A STAPLE THROUGH HER TUMMY, FOR A KICK OFF.

(UNLESS SHE'S GOT A PIERCED BELLY BUTTON!)

All pictures in magazines have been posed and the women have been heavily made up to look sexy. *— like me!*

Never forget that pornography isn't real –

it's fantasy.

❷ DON'T FEEL GUILTY.
Just because you got a copy of a girly magazine and used it to masturbate with, you are not a pervert. You're still going to be able to get it on with your girlfriend and you won't turn into a rapist.

dirty Mac brigade!!

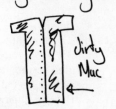

dirty Mac

LIKE MY TEAM WINNING THE FA CUP?

Some people feel that any form of pornography is exploitation, and that the women in the magazines and films are being used and abused purely for the *pleasure and gratification of blokes.*

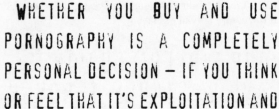

WHETHER YOU BUY AND USE PORNOGRAPHY IS A COMPLETELY PERSONAL DECISION – IF YOU THINK OR FEEL THAT IT'S EXPLOITATION AND WRONG THEN THERE ARE NO RULES THAT SAY YOU HAVE TO BUY IT.

However, the porn industry is one of the biggest in the world, making more money a year than all the Hollywood blockbusters put together, so that means there are a lot of people using pornography, not just you.

But what do you do if your mum finds your copy of **Big And Bouncy**?

THAT'S A LOT OF CASH!!

One thing is almost certain – she is not going to be happy. It might be that part of the fun of having a girly magazine in your room is that you have to hide it from **prying eyes**. It makes it all the more exciting because it isn't allowed.

However, that doesn't stop the fact that if it is finally found the sparks will probably fly.

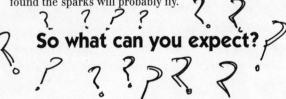

So what can you expect?

I'm different ←

Well, **everyone is different** and everyone's mum is different. Some mums might ignore it, some might choose just to bin the mag for you,

some mums will want to

talk about it and some mums will go

ballistic.

All these actions, and any in-between, are understandable – after all, you brought a dirty mag into your parents' house and they might not like that.

It's always best to remember two things when it comes to mums and magazines with pictures of women with no clothes on:

– no really?

(i) Your mum is a woman and a lot of women find any form of pornography highly objectionable.

(ii) Your mum is older than you and she might have different views on what is acceptable. What you feel is fine, she might find obscene.

A WORD OF WARNING

Looking at a magazine full of naked or beautiful women is easy. It's a lot easier than talking to a real girl, chatting her up, asking her out and trying to form a long term relationship with her.

If you are using porn there is **no fear of** *I prefer my*
rejection, no fear of being **hurt** – *girls to be*

you just pay your money and you've got *flesh and*

an instant *blood!*

two dimensional **girlfriend.**

But sometimes people let pornography replace real
relationships with *they are more*
squeezable!

GIRLFRIENDS OFF **real girls**
THE SHELF — with a
WHAT A **fantasy relationship**
GREAT IDEA!

with the perfect
women in the magazines. You shouldn't let it happen.
You might be getting your interests out of proportion if:

• you ever find your mattress is

getting so lumpy that you can't

sleep on it because of your vast

stash of girly magazines, or,

OH- ERMM – IS THIS
A BAD THING THEN?

112

- you find yourself more interested in spending every evening in your bedroom with Big And Bouncy magazine than going out with your mates.

Never - give me the real thing any day!!

( ) - fancy a snog J.C?

- not half.

Buying the occasional porn magazine is natural and fine. **Almost every bloke** has bought something that could be described as porn at some point in their lives.

You're not weird because you've **joined the club**.

But if it gets to the stage where you are buying several magazines at a time and have loads and loads of these things hidden away, then you might want to talk to someone about

why you prefer to look at *nudey pictures* **rather than talk to real girls**

BUT ISN'T IT GOOD TO HAVE A HOBBY?

– maybe you wouldn't want to talk to your mum or dad, but a brother, your GP or Childline could help. If you rely on porn rather than facing real girls, then you should try to stop.

I'VE GOT A GREAT COLLECTION OF MAGS WITH ERMM... ARTISTIC PICS IN THEM!

113

REAL GIRLS ARE MUCH BETTER:
THEY'RE PEOPLE.
THEY TALK.
THEY HAVE OPINIONS.
AND THEY LAUGH.

They're soft and cuddly and you can go on dates with them. When was the last time that you saw a guy taking his copy of Naughty Nymphs for a hot date down the local cinema?

and you can snog them

— kiss, kiss

WELL ACTUALLY THERE IS
THIS ONE REALLY WEIRD
GUY I KNOW WHO...

CHAPTER THREE

BOYS' MINDS BEHAVING BADLY

emotions

Lads have them. They might not like to think that they do – but they do. They feel

happy,

sad,

lonely,

angry,

bitter and

envious

I DON'T – BECAUSE I'M A REAL BLOKE!

I am a rock

see ↑

just in the same way that everyone else does.

But the thing with blokes is that they just aren't very good at expressing all these emotions. They bottle them up, push them down and try to ignore them.

– he, he, we can!

EMOTION – BOTTLED EMOTION – SPARKLING OR STILL?

It's all right for girls – they can get together with a few friends, watch a **soppy movie**, share some **secrets** and have a **hug** and a **cry**.

Lads don't do that.

Can you imagine phoning up your best mate and saying,

'I feel so sad, I want to cry. Will you hug me?'

It isn't going to happen.

HA, HA – WHO WOULD EVER SAY THAT??

116

HAPPY

SAD

DEPRESSED

WHAT IS DEPRESSION?

— it's when you press something!

Depression can mean just feeling sad and low for a couple of days or, in more serious cases, it can be a medical condition that needs treatment with either counselling or prescribed drugs.

So how can you tell if you are *— you feel squashed!*

depressed?

You feel sad and listless with little or **no energy**.

You might think that there isn't any point doing anything and you might feel isolated and alone. There is **NOTHING WRONG** with feeling like that for a week or so – but if those feelings go on longer or you feel down for a couple of weeks, happy for a couple of days and then down again – it's probably worth seeing your doctor about it.

like a see-saw

Why teenager have ups and downs

Anyone can become depressed, no matter what their age. You can be

70 or 17

great – so much to look forward to – good job I've got the babes to keep me happy!

and feel blue.

117

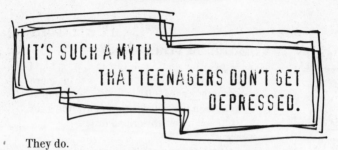

IT'S SUCH A MYTH THAT TEENAGERS DON'T GET DEPRESSED.

They do.

One in eight teenagers suffer from depression.
Many of them are lads.

Depression can be caused by almost anything and often there seem to be no reasons at all. A lot of teenagers get depressed because:

1. Puberty —again!!

One of the reasons that teenagers in particular can get

mood swings

and feel sad is to do with the

WELL AT
LEAST

hormone party that is puberty.

SOME
ONE

Puberty is a very unsettling time when your body goes through massive changes.

IS
HAVING A

GOOD

**Your hormones are having a party
all of their own inside your body.**

TIME

And the hormones don't just affect you physically, but they affect you emotionally too, with the result that you can go from feeling fine to feeling like the sky is about to fall in on you in a matter of minutes.

118

But hold on in there *because while you can still get depressed after puberty, once your hormones have begun to settle down, the sad feelings can also begin to lessen.*

THIS IS WHAT DEPRESSION LOOKS LIKE ←

2. Other reasons

Everybody is bound to get depressed if certain things happen, for instance:

* YOUR GIRLFRIEND DUMPS YOU,

* YOUR PARENTS SPLIT UP,

* YOU HAVE AN ARGUMENT WITH YOUR BEST MATE,

* YOU HAVE TO MOVE SCHOOL,

* SOMEONE CLOSE TO YOU DIES.

These things are always going to take time to get over.

So what can you do if things aren't going so great?

If you are **SAD** – you have to let it all out.

Bottle up feelings and you'll become an emotional pressure cooker ready to explode in a big sticky mess. According to doctors, if you bottle up emotions and deny them a release, you can make yourself physically ill. It's just not worth it. So how can you release them?

Yuk – THAT WOULD LEAVE A NASTY STAIN 😊

1. Cry – boo,hoo,hoo – ☹ – sometimes

What is it with *boys* and crying?

a few fake tears really win over the girls!

WE DON'T WANT TO LOOK LIKE GIRLS →

If you feel **UNHAPPY** and you have a **blub** it doesn't make you less of a man, it doesn't make you a big jessy or somehow weak. Blokes *are allowed* to be upset and vulnerable.

If you think being a real man is all about grinning and bearing it, you're wrong.

is getting of with loads of girls!

TRULY BEING A REAL MAN IS ALL ABOUT UNDERSTANDING YOUR EMOTIONS AND GIVING THEM A FREE REIN.

120

Been dumped – **have a cry.**

Your team out of the FA cup – **have a cry.**

Someone close to you died – **have a cry.**

Just feel down in the dumps – **have a cry.**

THAT WILL ALWAYS MAKE ME CRY!

2. Exercise

Sometimes, if you feel depressed, all you want to do is spend all day in bed or in your room with the curtains closed and dark and moody music playing.

However, it's been proven that one of the best things for depression is plenty of **exercise** and a **good diet**. If you spend all day in bed because you feel sad – you are more likely to feel *sadder* not *happier*.

of course – I have to keep my bod in good shape for the ladies.

Feel a little low?

I LOVE TO TALK – BUT ONLY ABOUT THE LATEST FOOTIE RESULTS

Go and run around a footie field – you'll probably feel a lot better.

3. Talk

It's really tough to talk about your emotions, but it's the best thing in the world if you feel sad and you just can't seem to stop yourself from feeling that way.

You might be surprised but just the

act of talking

to someone about a problem – even if they don't say
anything back to you –   **often helps**.

Just getting it off your chest, unloading and then
taking a **deep breath** and getting on with the rest of
your life is a great thing to do and it will make you feel
so much better.

So never think you are alone.

TALK TO PEOPLE.

GOLDEN DEPRESSION RULE:

 YOU FEEL CRAPPY

AND THAT FEELING WON'T GO AWAY?

 TALK TO SOMEONE.

Always remember:

- **Just because** you are a lad you don't have to
  bury your feelings of grief way down inside.

- **Just because** you are a lad it doesn't mean
  that you aren't allowed to feel sad and angry.

- **Just because** you are a lad it doesn't mean that you aren't allowed to cry, to break down and sob your heart out.

confidence

Having enough <u>belief</u> <u>in</u> <u>yourself</u> to put your ideas across, stand up and make yourself heard or just believe in what you want to do, can be a tough thing to master.

Everyone goes through patches of not being confident, of **doubting** their abilities or just doubting themselves in general.

And unless you get on top of it, it can **really ruin** your life because you'll find yourself missing out on so much.

Feeling:

- ○ **shy,**
- ○ **nervous around people,**
- ○ **inadequate,**
- ○ **insecure, or** // not me!
- ○ **unimportant,**

are all signs of a lack of confidence and they are more common than you might think.

EVERYONE SOMETIMES FEELS A LITTLE ROUGH!

that's me — I'm full of it! confidence that is!

123

What can be done about building your confidence?

You could start with a **LIST**.

It's not **dorky** and it's not **silly**
and no one ever has to know.

On one side of a piece of paper write down a list of the things about your personality that you might not like.

They might be:

- I'm shy,

- I'm not very good at speaking in class,

- I get embarrassed,

- I blush a lot,

- I'm envious of my little brother.

Mine would Just say "great guy"

WHAT IF YOU CAN'T WRITE?

?! - Dom!

124

You'll probably find it quite easy to come up with a

longish list.

I'd need another book to list the good qualities of J.C.!

That's not unusual – everyone finds it easier to come up with their bad qualities rather than their good ones.

Now, alongside your list of things you don't like, write down the things about yourself that you do like, to cancel out the bad stuff.

Write down one good thing for every bad thing that you've listed.

They might be:

I'm funny

I'm clever

I'm kind

I know... I know.

This will probably be tougher. Coming up with a long list of **good things** about yourself can be a

real challenge.

It doesn't mean that there aren't good things to find out about you – it just means that you'll probably have to look harder and

dig a little deeper.

FOR DIGGING

IM A GREAT MATE ... LOVE FOOTIE... WATCH TV ... EROM

125

If you are really having trouble coming up with enough, there is nothing wrong in **asking your mum and dad** what your good points are. You don't have to tell them that you are making a list – just ask them.

So you've got two lists of qualities, one next to the other –

some **good**,ıı ——— yup

YUP! ——— some **not so good**.

Now get the biggest, thickest, blackest felt pen you can find and cross out each bad point one at a time.

Really scrub them out.
Go at it hammer and tongs. like that?
Get rid of them,

so you can't see any of these things that you don't like about yourself.

SO YOU GET RID

OF ALL THE THINGS

YOU DON'T LIKE!

CLEVER!

Once you've done that you will be left with a list of good things. Positive things. Excellent things about yourself.

Fold up this list of your great qualities and put it in your pocket or in your wallet. Now, every time you feel lacking in confidence, get out the list and read all your good points.

IT DOES — It might sound silly. It might sound naff.

ALL SOUND RATHER SILLY! **BUT IT REALLY WORKS.** — *I've got all my old*

It's just a way or reminding yourself that you are a pretty neat person even if you don't feel it.

love letters from all the babes

What else can you do?

I've dated!!

If you worry about putting your ideas across because you think that everyone will laugh, just take a second and think: if someone else suggested this idea – would I laugh?

They remind me what a lurve god I am!

If the answer is **NO** –

why should anybody laugh at you if you make the same suggestion?

IF YOU WORRY ABOUT PUBLIC SPEAKING:

PRACTISE.

— the rain in spain falls mainly on the plain... I think I've got it!

127

Sit up in your room, close the door and... *and what?*

talk out loud.

Talk to yourself,

read the football results, say anything that you want.

MY TEAM 36, MANCHESTER UNITED 0,

Because
what you'll be doing is getting used to the sound of your own voice.

Most people don't really know what they sound like when they talk loudly in a quiet room. You sound different and it can be quite a **surprise**. If you've got a **speech** to make in class, a report or an interview fast approaching and it requires you to speak out loud and you know what you are going to have to say, there is nothing wrong with doing some **practising**.

Got to deliver a speech to the rest of your class?

Read through it out loud a couple of times beforehand. Get used to hearing your own voice say those words.

Again, you might think that this all sounds a bit daft.

YUP

BEFORE you go into an interview or

BEFORE you leave for a party or

BEFORE you stand up in class to give a report, there is nothing wrong with taking a **deep breath** and very **quickly saying** to yourself:

I'm great.

I'm good.

I'm pretty amazing.

I can do this.

I know what I'm talking about.

And everyone is going to be interested.

OK-OK — IM GREAT, IM WONDERFUL, BLAH, BLAH, BLAH, BLAH.

— all so true !!

IT WILL WORK.

It will help to built your confidence at the moment you need it the most.

— girls like to read my body language!

Body Language

And it isn't about what you say with your mouth, *— blah, blah, blah.*

but also what you say with your body.

Body language will express how confident you are as much as what you say.

POP QUIZ.

— who had a number one with....?

If you've got to meet someone important for the first time and you are going to be expected to shake their hand which of these is better?

A.

STRUTH!

Stand up straight, with your shoulders back and you head high. Grasp their hand firmly when you shake it and look them in the eye when you say hello.

SOUNDS LIKE YOU ARE IN THE ARMY — PRIVATE EDDIE!

B.

Shuffle in, slumped over and talking into the floor. Give them a limp handshake and mumble a hello over their shoulder.

The answer is A, of course.

party hats

You can use positive body language at **parties** too.

HERE'S A LITTLE SECRET:

THE HONE I KNOW ALL

GOALS MY TEAM HAS EVER SCORED — DOES THAT HELP?? ?

ask any girl what they find attractive in a guy and they will list a couple of things; **sense of humour, nice bum** and **CONFIDENCE.**

hey I've got all three — I must be so cool!

If you are going to a **party** remember that you've been invited because **you are interesting** and that someone wants you to be there.

When you **talk** to someone,

       look them in the eyes,

listen to what they are saying

      and you'll get on like a **house on fire.**

'what about my shades?'

95%

All stand up comedians say that of the trick in telling jokes, performing in front of a crowd and being funny is to do with confidence. If you are **CONFIDENT** (or seem to be confident) people will pick up on that and you'll go down a **WOW.**

HAVE YOU HEARD THE ONE ABOUT...

131

But what can you do if you get criticised after all this practising?

Coping with CRITICISM

Well that's wrong for a start.

Well, if you do some homework and it gets a bad mark, you tell a joke at lunch time and no one laughs or you try to explain something and it comes out all wrong *your confidence can suffer a real set-back.*

There is nothing more likely to **knock** someone's confidence that **criticism**.

No one likes begin criticised. However, criticism can be very **useful**. It can help guide you in your work and teach you when some actions are more appropriate than others.

GOOD CRITICISM ISN'T ABOUT PULLING APART SOMETHING YOU'VE DONE – IT'S ABOUT HIGHLIGHTING **STRONG** POINTS <u>AS</u> <u>WELL</u> <u>AS</u> WEAKNESSES.

like the fact that girls can't resist me – and that's a weakness?

If you are heavily criticised the only thing you can do is **go away and think about it.**

MY DOG'S GOT NO NOSE! HOW DOES HE SMELL? QUITE NICE – HE'S A VERY CLEAN ANIMAL. HA-HA!

132

(handwritten, left margin, vertical): IS A POWER GAME A BIT LIKE MONOPOLY?

(handwritten, left margin): I'VE GOT PARK LANE!!!

○ Ask yourself

why someone is criticising you.

Sometimes people use the chance to criticise to deliberately put someone down and make them feel insecure. It could be that they are **jealous** of you, or very **insecure** about themselves. It's a power game that some people like to play and you only let them **win** if you let their criticism affect you. You shouldn't. However, bear in mind that someone might be trying to help you, in which case:

(handwritten): — criticism is never right for me — because I'm so perfect.

○ Ask yourself

if the criticism is right.

A lot of criticism is based on **opinion**. Someone has disagreed with what you've said or done. If that person is important to you, and you trust their **judgement**, then it might be worth thinking about whether the criticism is **justified**. If it is not and you think what you've done is right and worthwhile – don't take any notice of them.

○ Ask yourself,

is the criticism criticism at all?

Sometimes you might be feeling very **paranoid**, and you take something someone says as a criticism, even when it isn't meant to be one. Like what? Well, say your mum says, 'Do you really like this music?' You might **mistake** that for criticism of your taste, when in fact it is only a

(handwritten): PARANOID? question.

(handwritten): ME? I'M NOT PARANOID! IT'S THE OTHERS — ALL OUT TO GET ME — I KNOW WHO THEY ARE. PARANOID — NOT ME!

Whatever you want to say or do you shouldn't ever let your own lack of confidence get in the way.

Practise,

take your time,

think about what you've got to do.

CONFIDENCE CAN BE LEARNT.

After all we all have something to say. It is just a matter of finding our own voice.

Unfortunately a lot of guys have trouble with a lack of confidence and instead of reading brilliant books like this one to find out how to make themselves more confident they depend on tricks to cover up their lack of confidence.

Which brings us neatly to the next chapter.

CHAPTER FOUR

BOYS BEHAVING BADLY WITH OTHER BOYS

peer pressure

← has this got something to do with the sea-side?

When lads get together, they sometimes do **silly** things. It's all part of being a bloke.

They egg each other on because they think they're being cool. They think whatever they are doing is going to impress the girls or they just want to look like tough men. *LIKE ME*

YEAH! THIS IS THE BIT I LIKE

What guys together do

They:

- **Make sexist jokes,**
  - **bully,**
  - **skip off school,**
  - **drink,**
  - **take drugs,**
  - **fight,**
- **brag about the number of girls they've been with.**

how many have you got? there have been loads - dozens, hundreds, thousands!

SO WHAT'S WRONG WITH ALL OF THIS?

These things might make you think you look good in the eyes of your mates or girls – but almost always they:

- make you look stupid, *– Doh!*
- **make you feel really ill, or even**
- **do long term damage to your body.**

YES! **So is it worth it?** NO

Will you still do them?

Probably.

Unfortunately that's what

blokes together can be like –

rather stupid. – *speak for yourself – that ain't me.*

BUT YOU DON'T HAVE TO BE.

WHAT – EVEN IF ITS LOADS OF FUN??

Saying, 'No'

It's difficult not to succumb to peer pressure. If everyone else is doing something, it's hard to say, 'NO'.

its not hard to say no

'NO' –

You might think you are going to be called a
~~big girl's blouse,~~ *I'd like to get inside a big girls blouse!*

a **party pooper**

or a **coward**.

OR IF THE FOOTIE IS ON

In fact, it takes a lot of courage and self control to say **NO** to your mates and people to whom you want to seem cool.

- You'd **rather** stay in with your girlfriend than go to the pictures with your mates **?**
  It can be difficult to **say no** but if that's what you want then you should.

  I'd rather stay in with u babe!

- You don't want to shoplift, even though all your mates are doing it, because you know it's **dumb**, **stupid** and **wrong**? It takes real guts to walk away from them.
  But think about it this way: if these people really are your mates and you really don't want to do something, then they should respect that. If they don't, and they do call you names, then they probably aren't such great friends.

**ALWAYS REMEMBER –
YOU DO WHAT YOU WANT TO DO.
DON'T AND YOU'LL REGRET IT.**

It's particularly

IMPORTANT

when it comes to things which can actually hurt you:

PILLS,
THRILLS
AND
BELLY
ACHES!

substances that make you feel great...

or not so great

— make mine a large pink gin!

booze

You might go to a party with the **belief** that if you have a drink you will automatically seem more **charming, attractive** and **funny** to all the girls in the room. You won't.

if I became any more charming, attractive or funny – I'd have to carry a government health warning.

Sooner or later most lads end up passed out in the **loo** with **vomit** all down their shirt and feeling like **death warmed up**. And then, after you have stumbled home, gone straight to bed, probably throwing up at least once more on the way, there is the next morning.

— WHY DOES VOMIT ALWAYS HAVE CARROTS IN IT??

You wake up feeling awful.

Your head **hurts.**

Your stomach **hurts.**

Your arms **and** legs **hurt.**

(handwritten: sounds like fun... not)

Everything **hurts.** ~~Everything~~

And then you remember what you did.

- You remember trying to put your hand up the jumper of that really cute girl from your maths class.
- You remember trying to get off with your best friend's mum, and,
- You remember drop kicking the cat across the garden.

(handwritten: HA HA HA. WHAT A LAUGH)

You look in the mirror and say to yourself,

'I'll never drink again.'

Why?

Why do we all put ourselves through it?

AGAIN IT'S MAINLY DOWN TO

PEER PRESSURE.

If all your mates are drinking,
then it must be something that
real men do.

If you can't hold your pints then you must be a bit of a big girl's blouse.

So what do you do?

Drink too much and fall over or not drink anything and get left out of the 'fun'?

BUT I DO WHAT EVER MY MATES DO!

BOOZE TIME OUT

tick tock tick tock

FIRST OFF,

IT'S ILLEGAL TO BUY ALCOHOL

IF YOU ARE UNDER 18,

so the problem shouldn't even come up. However, in the real world things aren't that simple and if you don't have your first drink until you're 18, you are very unusual indeed.

Is it only a choice of too much or nothing at all when it comes to booze?

No.
But it is difficult.

Hey, but I know when enough is enough - unless we are talking lurve - then enough is never enough!

141

The whole point about **alcohol** is that it affects your brain.

It **relaxes** you,

makes you feel more **free** and **easy**.

It gives you **self confidence** –

it makes you feel **funny** and **popular**.

it is hard to be cool and a lurve you if you've got the hiccups.

u-hic

IT ALSO AFFECTS YOUR JUDGEMENT.

so the **more** you **drink** the **less** likely you are to be able to **judge** when you've had enough. Which means you are likely to **drink more**, because you think you can handle it. Which will affect your **judgement**. Which means you are likely to **drink more**, because you think you can handle it. Which will affect your **judgement**. Which means you are likely to **drink more**, because you think you can handle it. Which will affect your **judgement**. Which means you are likely to **drink more**, because you think you can handle it. Which will affect your **judgement**. Which means you are likely to **drink more**, because you think you can handle it. Which will affect your **judgement**.

MY MATES ALWAYS TELL ME WHEN I'VE HAD TOO MUCH!

And so on and so on.

I'm a vicious circle!

142

But surely that isn't such a bad thing if it makes it easier for you to talk to people and makes you feel **more relaxed** or makes you **funnier?**

NOT TRUE.

The funny thing about booze is that it makes you **think** you are being **funny, charming** and **popular,** but you probably aren't. You're probably just being loud, **noisy** and **obnoxious.**

YA'!)) - like me!

THATS WHAT MAKES IT GREAT!

I'M THE PERSON INSIDE!

ALCOHOL DOESN'T CHANGE THE PEOPLE WE ARE INSIDE.

and I like who I am inside - I'm cool -

It's not a magic potion that will turn an unhappy and insecure person into a happy and popular one.

In fact,

different people are affected by alcohol in different ways. Some people just become very **giggly** and a little **silly** – others become **angry** and **aggressive.**

And never forget that if you do overdo it you are setting yourself up for all kinds of medical problems.

Like?

1. Hangovers

You have the fun – you pay the price. Hangovers **hurt**, they make you feel awful for days after your drinking spree.

They affect your ability to think straight and work properly. You feel **tired**, because when you are drunk you don't sleep properly, your stomach will feel **rough** and you might **throw up**, because alcohol in large quantities irritates the stomach lining, and your head will hurt because you, quite simply, **poisoned** yourself. If you are suffering from a hangover it's important that you rehydrate yourself because alcohol will suck the water out of your tissues, and you should eat loads of carbohydrates to help settle your stomach. **Beans on toast and cola are a great natural hangover cure.**

I FEEL TIRED IN THE MORNING ANY WAY!

YAWN!

beer belly! not for me - what would the girls say?

2. Beer Bellies

Drink too much and you will get fat. **Really fat.** Your stomach will distend and before you know it your tum will be hanging over your belt, and that is **not attractive**. Ask any girl.

COLA!

BEANS ON TOAST!

 - beer bellies! yuk!

144

3. Alcohol poisoning

If you drink too much booze in one go you can **poison** yourself. The body processes alcohol by absorbing it into the blood stream and then passing it round the body – that's how it gets to your **brain** and makes you feel tipsy. However, if you overload the blood stream with more alcohol than it can cope with you cause yourself problems. Then it could be off to the **hospital** to have your **stomach pumped** to get rid of any remaining alcohol there before it has a chance to get into the blood stream.

4. Liver damage

Drink too much for too many years and you will set yourself up for a whole load of problems in later life. Liver damage, also known as **cirrhosis**, is an illness directly linked with drinking. The liver is the organ in the body that cleans the **blood**. It's your in-built filter. If you pass too much alcohol through it over a period of years it will just pack up and stop working. And then you are in real **trouble**.

this is all very cheerful!

145

5. Strokes

Strokes are caused by haemorrhages in your brain. Blood leaks out and shuts down areas of your brain, or fails to make it to important areas of your brain and **kills** sections of it off. Not nice. Strokes can leave you **unable** to move, talk or walk. Although there are many possible causes for strokes, studies have shown that if you drink heavily you are more likely to suffer from one.

6. Alcoholism

Some people become **addicted** to booze. They don't just drink because it tastes nice or they enjoy it. They drink because they have to, because they can't get up in the morning without a drink, they can't leave their house without a drink, they **can't function** without a drink. Alcoholism is a very serious problem that can lead to all kinds of medical conditions and **depression** and in severe cases death. In most cases **alcoholism** creeps up on you and overtakes you. That's why no one should ever get drunk because they think it solves a problem, makes life easier or makes bad things go away. It doesn't. No matter what your worries or problems are, they will still be around after you have sobered up.

It's worth realising that research shows the drinking patterns we have as teenagers tend to be the drinking patterns we keep for the rest of our lives.

YOU GET INTO THE HABIT OF DRINKING

SO MUCH YOU THROW UP NOW

BUT IT'S VERY DIFFICULT NOT TO AT A PARTY - ESPECIALLY WHEN ALL YOUR MATES ARE GETTING WASTED.

AND YOU'LL PROBABLY DO IT FOR MANY, MANY YEARS TO COME.

There is nothing wrong with drinking. It tastes nice, it's social, lots of people do it. There isn't anything wrong with drinking a little bit too much. It's nice to feel tipsy and happy.

There is something wrong
with drinking so much that you pass out,
throw up or can't remember
what you did while you where drunk.

There is something wrong
with drinking because you can't face
a problem or because you think when you are
drunk you are a better or nicer person.

Always remember that moderation and self control are the keys. When it comes to drinking, a little is better than a lot and hangovers are really horrible.

↳ this has been a really heavy section of the book ↞ I don't half fancy a drink! - (Joke!)

147

cigarettes
↳ TABS, FAGS, SMOKES!

They might not be illegal if you are over 16, but cigarettes **can** and **do** KILL.

Smoking is a **disgusting** habit that only ever leads to bad and unpleasant side effects,

from the purely cosmetic:

stained fingers,
smelly clothes,
poor skin and
yellow teeth,
↳ not nice

to the terminal;

heart disease,
thrombosis and
lung cancer.
⇒ really not nice

Why do it?

Well, smoking can relax some people, making them feel more sociable and at ease. And some teenagers think it's cool and rebellious.

IT MAKES YOU LOOK "HARD"

have you ever snogged a smoker? — it's like chewing a pack of 20 - euk & c

But why?

What is so cool about

smelling like an ash tray

and what's so rebellious about

-yuk!

coughing up green slime

every morning?

Nothing.

However, smoking amongst teenagers is on the increase and it's down to that old problem of peer pressure. Ironically, the first time you smoke a cigarette it will taste disgusting. It might even make you throw up, but odds on you'll stand there with your mates, feeling awful, your eyes watering and say something like,

'hmmmm, that tastes great.'

But of course it doesn't.

Unfortunately smoking is highly addictive and any of the temporary pleasures that you gain from having a cigarette are very quickly replaced by a craving for more and more.

MMM-
NICE!.
SOMEONE
PASS ME
A
BUCKET!.

Ask any smoker who has been smoking for a number of years whether they would like to **GIVE UP** and almost all will say **YES**. Ask then why they don't and they will more often than not say that they can't.

IT'S JUST BEST NOT TO START.

drugs

— blimey, we really are getting into the heavy stuff!

There are a lot of drugs about and if you go to clubs or parties or just hang out it's more than likely that you will be offered some form of **illegal drug**.

If you are wondering what is meant by illegal drugs, well, they include, to name the most common:

THIS IS ALL A BIT SERIOUS!

Ecstasy,

Cocaine,

Cannabis,

Speed,

LSD

and Heroin.

a bit too serious to joke about!

No one can stop you from taking and experimenting with drugs.

HOWEVER, ALL THE ABOVE DRUGS ARE ILLEGAL FOR A REASON:

not to spoil your fun or to make life dull but because they do varying degrees of harm to your body. None of them are good for you in the long run.

Don't believe all the rubbish about some drugs making you happy all the time or giving you an insight into the meaning of life or being good for your soul. **THEY'RE NOT.**

They give you a quick pulse of pleasure and then can leave you feeling crappy for a long time. And, in the worst cases, they can leave you **DEAD**.

Is that a risk that you want to take?

But if you do get into the situation where you decide to experiment with drugs, just **stop** for a minute and **think**...

- Are you being pushed into it by peer pressure?
- Are you doing it because all your mates are doing it?
- Or because you think it will make you look cool?
    - Or because you think you have to because it's that type of party?
    - Or because you don't think you'll have a good time unless you do?
    - Or because you think it's fun to try anything once?

None of these reasons are good enough.

So what is there out there?

Glue Sniffing
and other dangerous substances.

These are not strictly drugs and not illegal to buy but they are **deadly substances** that can kill. When inhaled, certain glues, deodorants and aerosols create a floating, empty feeling. However, they are **addictive** and **dangerous**. After using them people are often sick and depressed. There are also a wide range of **breathing disorders** that can be caused by inhalation. The biggest danger of inhaling any form of glue or gas is that it's very difficult to regulate how much you are taking in and so it's very easy to **overdose** and you can do masses of damage to your lungs or even **DIE**.

Class A Drugs

All these drugs carry a maximum sentence of **7 years** in prison for possession and **life in prison** for selling or giving them away.

Ecstasy

Ecstasy is one of the major influences in youth and dance culture. It's sometimes simply called **E** and comes in a small papery tablet. It's associated with heightened perceptions and an overall feeling of warmth and happiness.

However, the combination of

ecstasy and hot clubs

can cause massive dehydration and heat stroke and it's not unknown for people to **collapse** after taking an ecstasy tablet.

They end up dehydrated

as they dance

for too long and don't

drink enough water.

Or they can drink **too much** water – in itself very dangerous.

> Studies have also indicated that ecstasy affects both the brain cells and liver causing long term damage if the drug is used regularly.

> After taking ecstasy it's very common to have a down time where users suffer from depression and listlessness.

ALWAYS REMEMBER:
ECSTASY CAN AND DOES KILL.

Cocaine

aka

charlie, horse, *snow*

Cocaine is a white powdery substance that, when snorted into the nose or smoked, can boost feelings of **excitement** and **confidence**.

However,

regular use of cocaine creates major heart and digestive problems. It's also linked to

paranoia, irritability and aggression.

COCAINE IS OFTEN ADDICTIVE AND CAN LEAD TO BOTH SOCIAL AND FINANCIAL DIFFICULTIES AS THE ADDICT WILL DO ANYTHING TO GET MORE COCAINE.

Crack is a stronger form of cocaine and is **highly addictive and highly dangerous.**

LSD
aka **acid, trips**

LSD is not dissimilar to ecstasy in appearance. It's also a chemical based drug that comes soaked in paper in small tablets.

Unlike ecstasy, it is a **hallucinogen.**

After taking it people feel other worldly and it can induce strange and disturbing visions. This is known as a trip. However, sometimes these trips can be extremely unpleasant and very scary – not unlike the worst and most believable **nightmare** that you've ever had. And once your trip has started you can't stop it until the drug has run its course, which if things go badly for you is extremely scary and unpleasant.

PROLONGED USE OF THE DRUG CAN LEAD TO FLASH- BACKS THAT CAN TAKE PLACE YEARS AFTER FIRST TAKING THE DRUG.

A flashback is where images from the drug induced experience appear unexpectedly, causing confusion and panic.

Heroin

HEROIN IS THE MOST DEADLY OF DRUGS.

IT'S FIERCELY ADDICTIVE AND EXTREMELY HARMFUL.

IT'S A DRUG THAT OFTEN LEADS TO DEATH.

It can be smoked or injected direct into the blood stream and due to the sharing of dirty needles can contribute to the spread of **HIV and AIDS.**

A temporary feeling of elation and extreme tranquillity is rapidly replaced by a desperate craving for more heroin as well as cramps, fevers, paranoia and sickness.

Class B Drugs

All these drugs carry a maximum sentence of **5 years** in prison for possession and **14 years** in prison for selling or giving them away.

Cannabis
aka weed, pot, tea, hash, grass, ganja

Using cannabis, which either comes in a resin or in a herb-like state, produces different effects on different people. It usually makes people feel relaxed, warm and sociable, but it can also produce feelings of anxiety, paranoia and panic.

Although the long term effects of cannabis aren't really understood, it's believed that when it's smoked in conjunction with tobacco it can cause
lung and throat cancer,
but that is as much down to the tobacco – a legal drug – as it is to the cannabis.
It's also thought that cannabis can spark off underlying **mental health problems**,
slow the reflexes and produce hallucinations.

Speed aka billy, wiz

Speed is a powerful stimulant that increases the **heart rate** and **body temperature** while removing the need for food or sleep. And while it can make people feel alert, communicative and talkative, it can also result in large mood swings, irritability and restlessness.
After using speed it's not uncommon to feel very depressed, tired and irritable.
And just like ecstasy, using speed in a hot club can lead to dehydration and heat stroke.

ALL FORMS OF ILLEGAL DRUG CARRY A HEAVY PRICE FOR THEIR USE.

And it's not just a **financial**

or legal price.

The brief pleasant sensations that all drugs create can leave you feeling like you **want more** of that **quick high**. The down time of depression, paranoia and panic gets longer as the good feelings get shorter, so it's not unusual to find yourself in a **downward**

spiral

of greater and greater drug use of more and more dangerous types of drug very quickly.

A lot of people will still, at some time or another, experiment with illegal drugs, no matter how often anyone has told them to just say no, no matter how often anyone is told that drugs are bad for them, no matter how often they hear horror stories of other people's bad, and sometimes fatal, drug experiences, but that doesn't mean you should.

AND ALWAYS REMEMBER:

because drugs are illegal people from whom you obtain drugs are involved in criminal activity, and are probably not to be trusted. One of the great dangers of drugs is that you might not get exactly what you think you are getting, but an even more dangerous mixture.

wow – that was all a little bit heavy – time for a laugh! ha ha ha!

⇒ ARE YOU STARTING!

fights 🏠 m-grr

The way you act around other lads can be heavily influenced by what your mates think and do.

It feels good to be part of a **gang** or a **clique**, to be surrounded by your mates and to feel their support when you get into a difficult situation.

Just bring me a gang of girls...

LISTEN MATE!

SOMETIMES

THINGS NEED

TO GET

SORTED!

It's all to do with safety: safety in numbers, safety in a group.

One for all and all for one.

hello ladies!

Unfortunately groups can have a downside. If you've ever got into a fight you'll know that it's usually all the people around the outside of the fight – often **your mates** – who are doing all the **cheering** and **encouraging**.

IT'S WHAT YOUR MATES ARE FOR!

It's them who are trying to get the fight going and make sure that the two people involved start slinging punches, **which is odd** – because if they really were your mates they'd try and stop you getting hurt in a scrap.

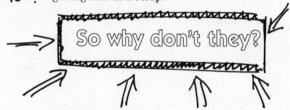

So why don't they?

159

Well, as a bloke it's still seen as an

act of courage

to get into a fight, to **square up** to someone and punch their lights out or, if necessary, **take a few punches** yourself.

BECAUSE THATS ⟶ **BUT WHY?**

WHAT
REAL
BLOKES
DO —
ISN'T
IT?

What's the point?

Usually if two people get into a fight it's over something really stupid and small.

How many times have you heard someone say:

- **He looked at me funny.**
- **I don't like his trousers.**
- **He said something about my mother.**

Are they GOOD ENOUGH reasons to square up and get physical with someone?

URM...
QUITE A
FEN — IN
FACT I
THINK I'VE SAID
MOST OF THEM!

NOT REALLY.

It's just all part of being male.

handsome
dude

I would never risk my good looks by getting into a fight!

Fighting time out

NO ONE who gets into a fight really wants to be there.

WHO WOULD?

You might get **hurt**, and no matter how **tough** you might like to think you are no one wants to go to school on Monday morning with a **black eye**. - you can't pull with a black eye!

Also, if after a fight you ask the two lads who were going at it hammer and tongs a couple of minutes earlier what all the **big fuss** was about, they'll probably not be able to tell you.

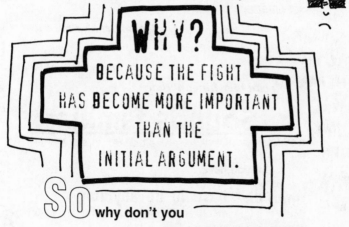

WHY? BECAUSE THE FIGHT HAS BECOME MORE IMPORTANT THAN THE INITIAL ARGUMENT.

So why don't you

just laugh off the fight,

maybe shoot a few angry glances

at the other guy and walk away?

- IT'S NOT THAT EASY - SOMETIMES YOU JUST HAVE TO SLING A FIST!

BECAUSE ONCE YOU'VE GOT INTO THAT SITUATION WHERE A FIGHT MIGHT BE IN THE AIR, YOUR SO-CALLED MATES TEND TO START EGGING YOU ON.

Did you hear what he just said about your mother?

Are you going to let him get away with that?

I wouldn't.

Go on, let him have it.

What are you afraid of?

I'd punch his lights.

You can take him anytime.

Sounds familiar?

It's almost as if you haven't got a say in the matter, isn't it?

But you have.

You **don't have to do anything** that you don't want to do. Even if your mates are trying to encourage you to start a fight –

you can always walk away.

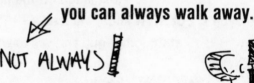

162

In fact,

it takes more courage to walk away from a fight than it does to start one.

thats what I think - and I'm very courageous

So that's one thing.

But what if someone squares up to you and decides that he wants to have a fight?

Surely then you haven't got any choice, it's a matter of defence? Well yes and no.

BUT IF SOME ONE HAS A GO AT ME — I'M NOT GOING TO JUST WALK AWAY!

If another bloke starts getting

aggressive,
getting his face into yours,
poking your shoulder
and generally 'asking for it',

you might think that is justification for making the first move. You could catch him on the hop and land him one on the chin. But then you haven't achieved anything. You've just got yourself into a fight that you didn't want to start in the first place, but now, because you made the first move, you've got to finish it.

So what else could you do?

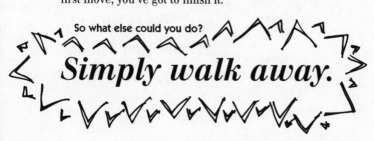

Simply walk away.

Turn around and walk away.

The guy who's picking a fight with you will probably do everything he possibly can to try and **provoke you.** He'll call you a **coward,** he'll try and start getting **physical** with you and he might even **punch** you.

But just like dancing cheek to cheek and making love, fighting takes two people to make it work. *= but it's not as much fun as dancing or making love! Bring on the girls!*

IF YOU SIMPLY REFUSE TO GET INTO A FIGHT — THE FIGHT WON'T HAPPEN.

Don't say a word, don't get into name calling or a slanging match, don't rise to the bait, just pick your stuff up and walk away.

~ THAT'S QUITE A "HARD" MAN THING TO DO!

164

To be able to **walk away** from a fight you have to be

LIKE ME! **strong.**

You might feel like a coward,

I feel like a snoy!!

you might feel like a chicken

and you might feel that you are running away.

BUT YOU'RE NOT.

It takes **huge** amounts of courage to walk away from a confrontation even though you know you might get more **respect** from your mates and more short term **glory** from getting into a scrap.

I BUT WHAT WILL YOUR MATES THINK?"

It's a bit of an old cliché from

sheriff JC — I always get my girl!

Saturday afternoon Westerns

– but the bloke who **refuses** to fight, even if he gets punched a couple of times, his ego gets bruised or he gets a black eye – is still the winner.

But it isn't just fighting that comes out of peer pressure. It's also bullying.

If you're a bully...

Don't think **bullying** is just something that happens at primary school with little kids stealing each other's sweet money.

> IT'S A PROBLEM THAT
> HAPPENS THROUGHOUT LIFE
> AND CAN CAUSE MISERY FOR THE
> PERSON WHO IS BEING BULLIED.
> IN EXTREME CASES IT CAN
> EVEN LEAD TO SUICIDE.

But what is bullying?

Well, it's getting at someone because they are different to you or your mates.

BUT I ONLY LIKE MY MATES!

166

- **If might be because they are smarter than you.**

  Or not as smart.

- **If might be because they haven't got as many friends.**

  Or dress differently.

- **It might be because they are disabled.**

  Or spotty.

- **If might be because they are of a different race or ethnic background.**

  In which case it's called racism.

- **If might be because they are effeminate or gay.**

  In which case it's called homophobia.

It can be for any reason

– but whatever reason it is, there is

absolutely no excuse

for being a bully.

Bullying is based on ignorance and fear, it's based on stupidity and prejudice and it's based on the, 'that person is different from me and my mates, he must be weird,' syndrome.

So how do you stop yourself from becoming a bully?

There is one
very
simple way.

LIKE ME! ⟶

Next time you and your mates are teasing someone, calling them names or just generally making their life less than pleasant – **just stop**.

Stop and think how you would like it, if it was you or *your best friend* or *brother* being picked on, being made to feel like you didn't belong, like you were a bit of a freak. *Just stop and think* how isolated and scared you might feel, how alone and desperate.

the word 'bully' is the same as the word coward – except it's spelt with completely different letters!

Stop bullying someone, stop making their life hell and give them back their self respect. You had no right to have taken it away from them in the first place.

Bullying time out.

Here's a question.

What's the difference between bullying someone and teasing them or taking the mickey?

TICK
TOCK
TICK
TOCK

Answer: Absolutely nothing if every time you see someone you tease them or take the mickey out of them.

No one minds being **ribbed** or being the **butt** of a joke from time to time but if you are always making someone the **punch line** of a gag, you are

bullying them.

It's a funny old thing but sometimes bullies **don't realise** they are bullying someone – they usually just think they are **having a laugh** and the only reason that their victim is getting upset is because they haven't got a **sense of humour**.

AND THAT IS SO WRONG.

Being bullied

Unfortunately it's not as simple to deal with being bullied. If someone is bullying you it can make your life hell. *– hell is having no girls around!!*

- **You don't want** to get up in the morning.

- **you don't want** to go to school.

- **you don't want** to go out.

- You feel **worthless**, **isolated** and **weird**.

- You begin to **believe** the bully's chants – you get called stinky enough times and you will begin to believe that you smell, even when you don't. *– and unloved!!*

So what can you *NO ONE* do if you are being bullied?

BULLIES EDDIE.

Well, you could try standing up to the bully – but unfortunately that rarely works. The bully is either part of a gang, and so he has safety in numbers or, like most bullies, he's been clever enough only to pick the times when he knows you can't do anything back.

MY MATES WOULD SEE TO THAT!

A BETTER TACTIC IS NOT EVEN TO TRY AND GET EVEN BUT INSTEAD GO AND TALK TO SOMEONE.

170

Your **mum** and **dad**, a **teacher**, anyone older than the bully who is in a **position of authority** and can do something to

STOP his anti-social behaviour would do.

NEVER THINK THAT JUST BECAUSE YOU ARE TELLING SOMEONE ELSE ABOUT THE FACT THAT YOU ARE BEING BULLIED IT SOMEHOW MAKES YOU A WIMP OR A COWARD. IT'S ALMOST IMPOSSIBLE TO DEAL WITH THE SITUATION YOURSELF.

Bullies are clever

because they often only pick on people who can't retaliate either because the bully is much older than they are or because the bully **holds a position of power** over the person that they are picking on.

It's not your fault hat someone is bullying you.

You haven't got the problem – *I never have problems unless you include which babies to have out*

they have.

They're the one

who is being anti-social and unpleasant.

OR TALK TO YOUR MATES

It's easy to say

– but much less easy to do –

but don't ever let a bully get you down.

They are only picking on you because they feel **insecure** about themselves.

It's true to say that bullies are **weak cowards** and deserve **no respect**.

Talk to someone and sort it out. You'll feel a lot better if you do.

J'c's order of things

1 – slugs
2 – worms
3 – creepy crawlies
4 – bullies

CONCLUSION

It's all up to you how you live your life.

It's your choice and your life. but always remember *I intend to be a little*

four things: *saint!!*

1. No matter how low, depressed, sad or broken hearted you feel,

THERE IS ALWAYS SOMEONE TO TALK TO.

All blokes feel upset and down and sometimes completely awful. There is nothing wrong with that.

2. Puberty is a *roller coaster ride* and sometimes the best policy is just to hang on and close your eyes.

I GET SICK ON ROLLER COASTER RIDES!

From shaving to girls to masturbating to feeling depressed to discovering your sexuality,

things can seem confusing and bleak. But your body knows what it's doing – trust it.

3. Once you become an adult, things don't get any easier or simpler. You don't hit 20 and all of a sudden have all the

174

answers. It would be nice if that was the case – but it isn't. For the rest of your life things can sometimes seem confusing, bleak and difficult. But don't panic, because most of the time everything works out in the end.

4.
You are a wonderful person.

There is no one like you anywhere else in the world.

You're special – never forget that.

- IS THAT IT?
IS THAT THE END?

I guess so!
Good book I thought -

- YER - BUT I THOUGHT
THE BUTLER DID IT!

Nav that's the sequel!

THE END